The
Ingenio
Mr Pedersen

Mikael Pedersen (R.A. Lister & Co. Ltd. collection)

The
Ingenious
Mr Pedersen

David E Evans

ALAN SUTTON

Alan Sutton Publishing Limited
Phoenix Mill, Far Thrupp
Stroud, Gloucestershire

First published 1978

Edition with new appendix and additional illustrations published 1984

First published in this paperback edition 1992

ISBN 0 7509 0064 4

Typeset and origination by
Alan Sutton Publishing Limited.
Photoset Times Roman 10/11.
Printed in Great Britain.

Contents

Dedicated to all the friends I have made through cycling.

Foreword

The Dursley Pedersen bicycle was perhaps the most remarkable design of machine in the long history of the bicycle. It appeared just before the turn of the century and therefore enjoyed all the benefits of the pneumatic tyre, roller chain drive, ball bearings etc. The unique feature of the Pedersen, which gave it its distinctive appearance and behaviour, was the use of small diameter thin-walled tubes in a triangulated structure of great lightness to support the comfortable hammock saddle. It rightly attracted much attention and support among the discerning cyclists of the day. No doubt there were some who thought that the future of bicycle design lay with the Pedersen rather than the Starley Safety, which had become definitive at about the same period. However it was the simplicity of manufacture of the larger-tube machine together with its general ruggedness and stiffness that resulted in the Starley principles becoming ubiquitous for more than half a century, while the more exotic design only survived on the market for a couple of decades. Luckily many examples survive today lovingly restored and ridden by veteran cycling enthusiasts. Indeed it is not impossible that some features of the construction of the Pedersen will be revived for incorporation in a modern machine.

In this first published account of the life of Mikael Pedersen by David Evans we can read the fascinating story of how a prolific inventor established his manufacture in Dursley, Gloucestershire, through the entrepreneural help of the Lister family. To one who has unwittingly trodden a somewhat similar path in the bicycle field many of the events have a familiar ring today! We read of the machine being taken up and publicised by the personalities of the day, records being established with it and even demountable versions being made for military use. It is also easy in retrospect to understand how the inventor over-estimated the commercial value of his creation in the scale of royalties required. To me the most appealing aspect of the Dursley Pedersen venture was the quality of workmanship and attention to detail design that the machine displayed. For this I suspect we are indebted to Mikael's assistant A.E. Mellerup. Examining one today, which has come into my possession from Lord Methuen, one marvels at how well the thin tubes have survived for seventy years, and how light and elegant are the lugs.

To those of us who are interested both in the history of the bicycle and in the vicissitudes of establishing an innovation on the market, we must be indebted to David Evans for his painstaking research and lively narrative displayed in this book.

Alex Moulton, C.B.E.,

The Hall, Bradford on Avon.

Introduction

The Dursley Gazette for 21st October 1893 reported:—
"A New Bicycle.
"Mr. M. Pedersen of Dursley, with that ingenuity for which he is known, has recently constructed a safety bicyle of remarkable character. Its weight is only nineteen pounds and the maker has tested the strength in an extra-ordinary way, he having ridden it up Whiteway."

Whiteway is easily described. It is the long snaking 1 in 7 hill that carries the main road to Tetbury from the town of Dursley, set on a shelf 200 feet above the Vale of Berkeley, up another 350 feet towards the level of the Cotswold Plateau. It is part of what Gloucestershire racing cyclists call the 'Dursley Ladder' and in 1893 it would have been surfaced with rain washed gravel. In 1896 it was considered sufficiently steep by the Cyclists Touring Club for it to instruct Mr. Bird, a local wheelwright, to erect warnings — "Notice to Cyclists. This Hill is Dangerous."

Who was this ingenious Mr. M. Pedersen who could ride up such a hill and what was it about his safety bicycle that made it so remarkable?

My first sight of a Dursley Pedersen cycle came many years ago in Exeter when an American fellow student returned excitedly with one from an auction. Apart from a cursory look at what was obviously a cycle of unusual design I took no great interest in it but the name stuck.

In 1968 I moved to Dursley and found quickly to my surprise that this was the town of the cycle's name and that the machine was remembered and talked about with something approaching affection by local people as one of the great features of the community's past. My interest was kindled and from then on I gathered information about the bicycle and its inventor.

Most difficult to find out were the facts of Mikael's life before and after his 30 or so years in England. A break through came when I discovered in the membership list of the Southern Veteran — Cycle Club, the name of FINN WODSCHOW of Copenhagen. I contacted Finn and found that he too was interested in Mikael Pedersen and that he had managed to obtain a 1909 Dursley Pedersen Cycle, the only one to this day — so far as is known — in Denmark. Finn has a grand collection of veteran cycles and they were displayed a few years ago in the window of a Copenhagen bank. The Pedersen machine brought to Finn's door Vagn Jensen, one of Mikael's sons.

Correspondence between Dursley and Copenhagen came to a climax in November 1977 when I was able to travel to Denmark to meet Finn and Agnes, Vagn, Toke — another of Mikael's sons — and Mrs. R. Adelbrandt, a niece of Mikael. As a result of the great kindness of these Danish folk, a reasonably complete story of Mikael's life can be told.

What follows is the result of many years of fascinating research and if it informs about one of the most famous of veteran cycles and about the remarkable man who was its inventor, it will serve a useful purpose.

From time to time costs and prices are quoted. To turn these into present day values is difficult but if one multiplies such figures by ten the magnitude at least will be indicated.

Cycling exploits are mentioned at times. It should be born in mind in considering these that asphalting of roads was not common until well into the first decade of this century and then it was largely confined to the more major thoroughfares. Thus the majority of rides touched upon took place on roads, dusty or muddy by turn, and stoney, rutted or potholed in varying degrees.

Unless otherwise stated, quotations are from the 'Dursley Gazette' of the period.

David E. Evans

Dursley, Gloucestershire
1978.

Acknowledgements

I acknowledge with great pleasure the help I have received from the following people:—

Denmark
    Finn Wodschow and Agnes, Copenhagen, whose hospitality I shall always remember.
    Vagn and Toke Jensen, Copenhagen ⎰ who greatly honoured
    Mrs. R. Adelbrandt, Copenhagen ⎱ me by their confidence.
    Eva Tonnesen, Archivist, Bibliotek, Roskilde.
    Svend Nielsen, Director, Landbrugsmuseet, Auning.

Dursley
    The Proprietors and Mr. D. Archer, Editor, and his staff, The Gloucestershire Gazette Series of Newspapers, for their generous permission to make extensive use of their files and for their unfailing courtesy and helpfulness.
    Messrs. R.A. Lister & Co. Ltd. for their permission to print many pictures from their photographic collection.
    Mr. D. Asher, Publicity Manager, and Major D. Gale, Training Officer, R.A. Lister & Co. Ltd., for being so helpful and patient with my enquiries.
    Miss V. Rodway, assisted by Mrs. M. Gunston, for deciphering and typing what I had written.
    Mr. C. Howarth of Uley, who did much of the initial photographic work.
    Mr. C. Adams, Mr. B. Ashworth, Mr. E.K. Benjamin, Mr. G. Cross, Mr. R.J. Harper, Mrs. D. Hearn, Mr. A. Hollingsworth, The Rev. E. Hoskin, Mr. S. Marshall, Mr. P. Neale, Mr. J.P. Sirett, Mr. A. Sutton, Mrs. L. Trollope, Mrs. Vines, Mr. B.S. Webb for providing information, photographs and help in other ways.

Southern Veteran-Cycle Club
    Mr. W. Bush, Mr. G. Clarke, Mr. G.W. Hall of T.G. Hall Cycles, Gloucester, Mr. R.F. George, Mr. A. Paris, Mr. J. Pinkerton and many others for help and interest.

Mr. R. Currie, Midlands Editor, and Mr. J. Clew, writer, "Motor Cycle" magazine.

The Editor and Mr. P. Knottley, writer "Cycling" magazine.

Mr. Ben Ashworth of Churchdown, Glos.

Mrs. L. Balman of Reading.

Mrs. V. Rees of Portishead.

The County Archivist and his staff, County Records Office, Gloucester.

Mr. C.T. Jones, Sales Director, Wolseley Webb Ltd., Birmingham.

Mr. A. Jewell and his staff, The Museum of English Rural Life, Reading.

Alex Moulton, like Pedersen, a great innovator in cycle design, for his help and encouragement.

Mrs. M. Tucker, Uley for assistance with Mikael's music.

Chapter One
Mikael Pedersen comes to England
1855-1899

Mikael Pedersen was born on 25th October 1855 in Denmark at Flong near Marbjeg, between Copenhagen and Roskilde. He was the eldest of seven children, 3 girls and 4 boys. Like his grandparents, his parents were farmers in the Marbjerg area though after the children had grown up they had to sell up through standing as guarantors for a large sum of money for a neighbour who proved to be a bad risk.

Of his brothers, Ole Hans became a priest in the Lutheran Church, Hans became an orchestral conductor and Peter established himself in the clothing trade. One sister, Mary had a shop in Frederiksuund, and a second married an Irish dairy farmer.

Mikael seems to have been an inquisitive, inventive child, gregarious by nature. By the time he was 14 years old he had joined the local band and soon became an accomplished performer on string and wind instruments. In time he became the leader and used to borrow his father's cart to transport the band to weddings and other festive occasions.

On leaving school he became an apprentice at the Maglekilde Maskinfabrik of Roskilde — a factory producing agricultural equipment. Mikael seems to have stayed with this company for some time and perhaps it was while here that he began inventing on his own account such items as a self clearing threshing machine which he hired out to local farmers.

One invention was a uniquely shaped bicycle. For many years Mikael had been a cyclist, first on ordinary ("penny farthing") cycles and then later on smaller wheeled 'safety' machines. With a critical eye he saw, or perhaps he felt, that great improvements could be made, particularly in the saddle. Thus the hammock saddle was evolved and as this didn't fit easily on the cycles of the day, Mikael developed a triangulated frame to take it. The metal parts of this were fabricated at the Maglekilde factory in Roskilde. This

Denmark

RANDERS

MARJBERG COPENHAGEN

ROSKILDE

0   50   100

MILES

new bicycle later became known as 'The Dursley Pedersen'.

In 1878, when Mikael was 23 years old, the Maglekilde factory began to make an item which was to be of profound significance for him — a centrifugal cream separator.

The age old way of separating cream for butter making was to allow milk to stand for a while and then skim off the surface cream. It was a slow intermittent process and considerable research was done in the second half of the nineteenth century to develop an efficient continuous and more rapid process. The Maglekilde design was one of the first to approach the ideal.

In the centrifugal machine, milk is fed into a bowl rotating at high speed. Under centrifugal forces the milk separates into two layers, cream and whey, which are bled off separately. For maximum efficiency the bowl must spin at a constant speed — something that was difficult to obtain with the horse and hand drives then available. Mikael saw a way of overcoming the problem. He designed a machine in which the bowl sat loosely on a ball head. The head was turned by horse or hand power and in turn, by friction, span the bowl. Once spinning the bowl's momentum smoothed out any fluctuations in the speed of the ball head. This idea Mikael is said to have got from watching a circus performer balancing plates. So smooth was the action of his machine that the separator no longer needed to be fixed to the floor.

Mikael took his design to Jens Nielsen, owner of the nearby Roskilde Maskinfabrik in 1885. The two men patented the idea in Denmark and Sweden and began manufacture. In 1886 the manufacturing rights were bought by the Copenhagen firm of Koefoed and Hauberg for marketing on a world wide scale.

Mikael seems to have gained well financially and became a relatively rich man. In Marbjerg in 1888 he built a house of his own design which was unusual in that it had a large central "festsal", or room for entertaining, which was surrounded by small rooms. By this time Mikael was married to Laura.

The house still stands (1978) in Marbjerg though much altered internally. It was occupied by soldiers in the First World War. They broke into the loft where many household items were stored and used much as firewood — including many of Mikael's prototype inventions.

In England, Robert Ashton (later Sir Ashton) Lister, as a young man had set up in 1867, in Dursley, Gloucestershire, a small iron foundry and workshop for producing farm equipment. By the 1880's the firm was becoming well known, partly because of the

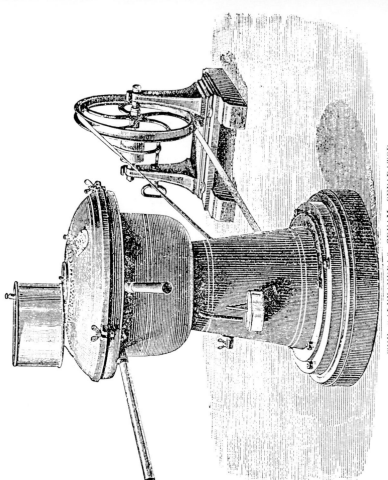

THE "ALEXANDRA" CREAM SEPARATOR.

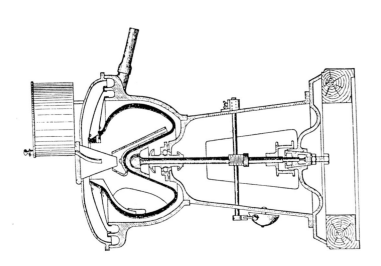

high quality of the wares and partly because of R.A. Lister's tours at home and abroad. It is likely that Mikael met him on one of his Danish tours and Mr. Lister, realising the possibilities for Mikael's cream separator in England, gained the British selling rights from Koefoed and Hauberg. Thus the famous Lister "Alexandra Separator" came into being. It first appeared in 1889 in England, shortly after the silver wedding celebrations of the Danish born Princess Alexandra and the then Prince of Wales, and in the next ten years did more than any other of Lister's products to bring about the tremendous growth of the firm in the 1890s.

Mikael Pedersen came to England in 1889 and attended the December Smithfield Show. The "Implement and Machinery Review" commented on the equipment that was on display and after noting that R.A. Lister & Co., had Alexandra Separators on their stand said:— "The inventor Mr. Petersen (sic) was present and is associated with Messrs. Lister's staff. They have in him a practical buttermaker and a man emminently qualified to assist to a very successful issue the dairy machinery section of their business ....." (Implement and Machinery Review Jan. 1890)

Quite when Mikael came to live in England is not certain though the evidence points to early 1893.

Why he came is also uncertain. It is possible that he was invited to by R.A. Lister who felt, perhaps, that Mikael might produce some more good ideas. In later years Listers did market an "Alexandra Horse Gear" and an "Alexandra Butter Moulder" and these may have been Mikael's inventions. Certainly the two men kept in contact as Mikael was associated with R.A. Lister in attempts to overcome the restrictions resulting from having the patent rights of the Alexandra Separator vested in Koefoed and Hauberg, restrictions that R.A. Lister found irritating to say the least.

Edward, eldest son of R.A. Lister, in 1889, advertised himself as an agent for Humber Cycles and as having "laid in a stock of cycling requisites".

Perhaps Mikael saw the Lister family as having interests akin to his own and having, it is said, received little encouragement from Danish companies for some of his inventions, this prompted his move. The only certainty is that move he did. His wife Laura did not accompany him and it is possible that it was about this time he divorced her.

With him he brought the design for his novel triangulated bicycle and to the development of this machine he now turned his attention.

Dursley at about the time Mikael arrived. Long Street — Kingsley and Raglan

......and Parsonage Street. Long Street goes off to the left of the Market House.

South Gloucestershire

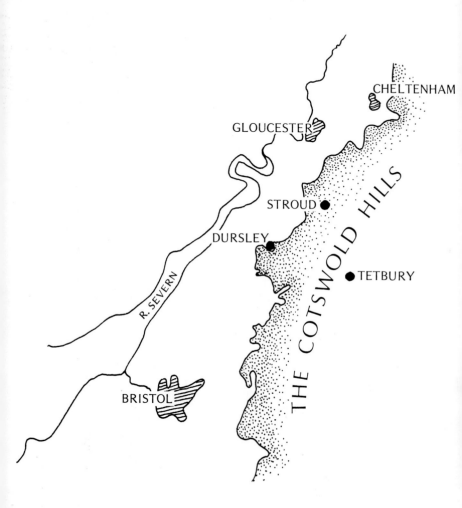

CHELTENHAM

GLOUCESTER

STROUD ●

DURSLEY ●

TETBURY ●

R. SEVERN

THE COTSWOLD HILLS

BRISTOL

0   5   10

MILES

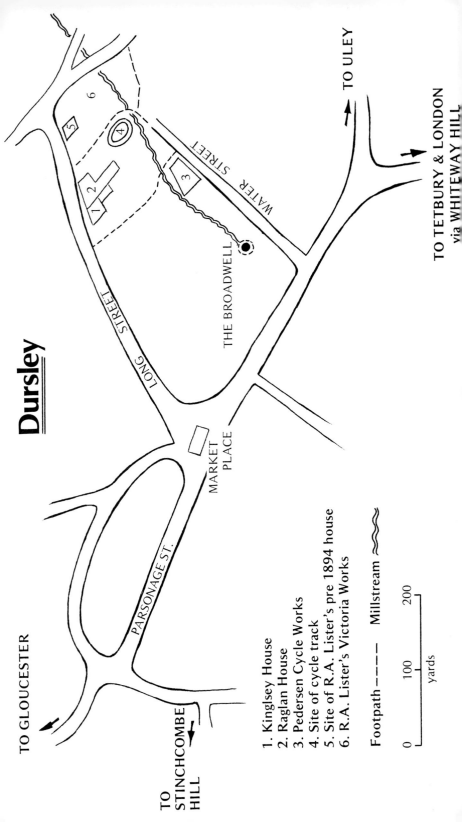

Dursley

TO GLOUCESTER

TO STINCHCOMBE HILL

PARSONAGE ST.

LONG STREET

MARKET PLACE

WATER STREET

THE BROADWELL

TO ULEY

TO TETBURY & LONDON via WHITEWAY HILL

1. Kinglsey House
2. Raglan House
3. Pedersen Cycle Works
4. Site of cycle track
5. Site of R.A. Lister's pre 1894 house
6. R.A. Lister's Victoria Works

Footpath – – –   Millstream ∿∿∿

0   100   200

yards

By March 1893 he was well established in Dursley. He was certainly not a poor man. He occupied a large house, Kingsley House, in Long Street very near the Lister Factory; he was one of only seven people, mainly members of the Lister family, who were the first shareholders in R.A. Lister & Co. Ltd. having £500 worth of shares, increased in 1896 by another £1155 worth; in September he applied for a patent for his cycle and, judging from the newspaper report quoted in the Introduction, was well known.

As was to be expected of a man who loved company, he became popular quickly and in November was one of a number of singers who entertained the town at one of the regular popular Saturday Concerts at the Victoria Hall. Other singers were Austin, one of R.A. Lister's sons, and Mr. Ashworth who in later years was commercial manager of the cycle works. Also present was the 'Dursley String Band'.

In the following year, 1894, Mikael visited Denmark, taking with him a Pedersen cycle and returned later to England with a newly and highly qualified engineer Anders Eiler Mellerup, who was to be his right hand man for many years. In this year too he patented his cycle in Denmark, Sweden, Belgium and France.

Early machines were largely of wood and it was not until about 1897 that this material was finally abandoned for metal tubing. The first all metal machine was made in about 1896, heralding, or part of, a great expansion of activity on Mikael's part.

In 1896 he applied for a patent on his methods of jointing the metal frame. He joined as a partner an established firm of engineers, machinists and millwrights in Ashton Gate, Bristol which as Humpage, Jacques and Pedersen lasted until 1907. With Mr. Humpage and Mr. Jacques, Mikael in April attended a conversazione connected with the extension of the University College (now University) held at the Victoria Rooms in Bristol. His bicycle went too and excited much comment. "Mr. Pedersen appears to have happily solved the difficulty which has long perplexed cycle makers, who have for years, been endeavouring to discover how to manufacture roadsters in a manner which combines phenomenal lightness and requisite strength." In this year too Ernest Terah Hooley came on the scene. Opulent, colourful, "the millionaire of cycle and Bovril fame", financier of Chicago, Hooley offered to float a £¼m. company to market the Pedersen cycle. Agreement was reached in November for Mikael to sell his invention and patents to Hooley for £3000 and for Mikael to act as a Director and Factory Manager in the proposed 'Pedersen Cycle Frame Co. Ltd.'

N° 18,371

A.D. 1893

Date of Application, 30th Sept., 1893
Complete Specification Left, 2nd July, 1894—Accepted, 4th Aug., 1894

PROVISIONAL SPECIFICATION.

Improvements in or connected with Bicycles.

I, MIKAEL PEDERSEN, of Kingsley House, Dursley, in the County of Gloucester, Engineer, do hereby declare the nature of this invention to be as follows :—

My invention relates to bicycles and has for its object to construct the frame 5 in such a manner that a frame calculated to carry a given weight may be made much lighter than heretofore.

According to my invention the frame comprises a portion (hereinafter referred to as the rear wheel bracket) composed of two parallel or nearly parallel bars, one end of which carries the journal or bearing of the rear or driving wheel whilst the 10 front end carries the journal or bearing for the pedal shaft. To the front end of the said rear wheel bracket adjacent to the pedal shaft bearing are connected three forked frame sections, two of which are connected with the front wheel fork and are supported thereon in such a manner that the said fork can be turned for the steering of the machine. The third of the said frame sections extends rear- 15 wards into such a position that it serves, in conjunction with a forked stay extending from the rear end of the rear wheel frame, for supporting the seat which is suspended between the ends of the third frame section and stay.

In order that the weight upon the seat shall not draw the suspension points of the saddle too close together a light bar, wire, cord or the like is attached to the 20 extremity of the said third frame section and to the rear end of the rear wheel bracket at each side of the wheel.

The front wheel fork is composed of two double triangular parts, or of two single bars, suitably connected together at or near the centre of their length and united at their upper ends.

25 In the case of a machine adapted for use by men the upper end of the front wheel fork is jointed to the point at which the seat stay and the central forked frame section meet.

In the case of a machine intended for use by ladies where it is necessary to provide considerable space between the seat and the steering fork, the said stay, 30 from which the front end of the seat is suspended, is not connected to the top of the steering fork, in which case additional triangular struts are provided extending from the rear end of the rear wheel frame to the third frame section, thence to the second or central frame section, and thence to the extremity of the first or front frame section.

35 The handle bar is preferably attached to the front wheel fork so low down that it will cause as little twist as possible of the front wheel fork when steering the machine and at the same time serve as a foot rest.

My improved frame may be made of metal or partly of wood and partly of metal.

40 I may in some cases provide suitable struts from which a second seat may be suspended to form a tandem bicycle.

The saddle which I advantageously employ is composed of a series of cords or strings at one end connected to a bent bar and at the other end to a common point.

45 Dated this 30th day of September 1893.

G. F. REDFERN & Co.,
4, South Street, Finsbury, London, Agents for the Applicant.

[*Price* 8*d.*]

Provisional specification of patent of Sept. 1893 (G.R.O.)

The company was formed on 16th December 1896 and Mikael's fellow directors were Lord Walter Lennox and H.C. Richards M.P. A building was acquired in Water Street, Dursley for £1050. This was the factory of the Victoria Pin Company, then recently rebuilt and well lit, with steam engine, ample water power from the little Broadwell Stream and containing complete plant for nickel plating.

In spite of being so busy he found time for social activities and took an interest in sport. There is no evidence to show that he ever played team games in the town but his cycling exploits indicate that he enjoyed physical activity. In March 1896 he was elected with cheering to the Presidency of the Dursley Star Rugby Football Club for the 1896-7 season and three weeks later was elected President of the Dursley Star Cricket Club.

In the spring of 1897, Pedersen, helped by A.E. Mellerup, five skilled mechanics and a lad began to produce cycles. Initially it seems that the main aim of the Pedersen Company was not to produce many cycles in Dursley but to induce other manufacturers to do so under license. The Water Street premises could perhaps best be described at this time as an inventor's workshops.

Other manufacturers were found to be interested in the Pedersen cycle. Trent, Singer, Valkyrie, Brooks, Monopole and particularly Humber produced Pedersen cycles and exhibited these at the Stanley and National Cycle Shows at the end of 1897. The Pedersen Cycle Frame Co. also had a stand. However, reviewers of the period were generally critical of the cycle and it is likely that very few of these 'under license' Pedersens were made or sold.

The foreign market was not ignored. 'The Hub' for 26th June 1897 stated that it had heard that "a new machine called the 'Pedersen' had been placed on the continental market." In the U.S.A. patent license was granted in February and a company promoted to manufacture the cycles.

Mikael Pedersen changed houses, moving next door into Raglan House, the grandest house in Long Street with more rooms and with a large garden in which he laid out a private cycle track. His inventive talents were now fully unleashed and before the end of the year (1897) he had applied for patents to cover

a) improvements to "crank axles and bottom bearings" to reduce weight and the degree of adjustment needed

b) improvements to pedals, making them lighter and "less liable to injury"

c) the construction of tandems and triplets which, when made, excited considerable interest.

"At the Pedersen Works, Dursley ...... we recently saw a tandem

Mikael Pedersen and one of his sons outside Raglan House, Dursley about 1914
(Toke & Vagn Jensen)

The garden of Raglan House soon after 1893. Just visible is the cycle track and beyond the far corner can be seen early buildings of R. A. Lister's Victoria Works

Inside Raglan House — probably about 1914 (Toke & Vagn Jensen)

The mill buildings that were the Pedersen Cycle Works in Dursley. Looking down

Looking up Water Street. The stream emerges from the right side of the mill (C. Howarth 1977)

machine ...... It was a splendid piece of workmanship and reflects credit upon all concerned.''

Mr. Percy Ashworth, son of W.J. Ashworth, for many years Commercial Manager of the Pedersen Works, recalled riding as a youth on a triplet to Gloucester and back with Pedersen and Mellerup. Although pedalling as hard as he could he was castigated by the others for a lack of effort which reduced their speed!

A four seater 'Quad' was built and exhibited in the 1898 National Show. "It is a really beautiful piece of mechanism and it has the merit of being at least 80lbs lighter than any similar machine made. It is exactly on the same principle as the single machine and is a valuable 'eye opener' to racing men and experts generally.''

Optimism in these years must have been high in the Water Street works. Extra men were taken on and although the cycling press was largely hostile the local newspaper recounted with enthusiasm every development.

"The Pedersen bicycle, the manufacture of which bids fair to become an important industry in Dursley, has attracted considerable attention on account of its novel appearance, the inventor having had little consideration for the cherished ideas of other makers as regards its construction. There is no doubt about this — that all who have ridden the new machine in which strength is combined with minimum weight, speak of it as being the ideal cycle in point of comfort. The other evening Mr. Mellerup, an employee at the works accomplished on the Pedersen machine, a feat which has hitherto been considered an impossibility, when he rode up Stinchcombe Hill with comparative ease without once dismounting, despite numerous ruts in the road. This speaks volumes for the wonderful stability of the machine. The route chosen for the performance was the ordinary one from Parsonage Street'' (which is about 1 in 4 in places!)

Other periodicals commented favourably too, particularly on the saddle. "The Pedersen saddle is of string partaking of the elastic character of a net or hammock. Surely this is the thing we want. The same saddle will accommodate itself to all sizes of cyclists and produces none of those awful aches and pains which are the besetting sin of other saddles.'' (National Football News).

Anders Mellerup was one of at least two budding cyclists on the Pedersen Company staff, the other being Jens Jorgensen, another Dane. Both men took part in Dursley's Annual 'Athletic and Cycling Sports' in 1897 when Anders came 3rd in the one mile novices grass track race and 1st in the handicap one mile race for local people. Jens Jorgensen came 3rd in this. The sports yearly

Mikael and Dagmar on the Raglan House track, about 1898 (R.A. Lister & Co. Ltd. collection)

PEDERSEN TEAM (MR. JORGENSEN LEADING, MR. MELLERUP THIRD FROM LEFT) BEING PACED BY MR. PEDERSEN, THE INVENTOR

Members of the 'Pedersen Cycle Club' on the Raglan House track, about 1898. It is likely that on the quadruplet, No. 2 is Mr. Rasmusser and that No. 4 is Austin, son

attracted hundreds of cyclists from miles around and programmes listed such defunct Clubs as Cheltenham Million, Cheltenham Quianton, Gloucester Tyndale, Bristol Wheelers, Bristol North, Bristol Richmond, Tewkesbury and Cinderford Cycling Clubs as well as Bristol South C.C., happily still with us. Obviously such gatherings were ideal for advertising the Pedersen cycle and Mikael took heed, though Mellerup did the work!

"Success on the Racing Path.

The 'Pedersen bicycle's first appearance in an open handicap created at Stroud Sports on Whit Tuesday (1898) quite as great a sensation as did the first pneumatic tyres on the Dursley Track some years ago when it carried all before it. The machine, which weight about 17lbs, was ridden by A.E. Mellerup of Dursley who had never been in an open race before. Consequently he was given a start of 45 yards from the nearest opponents in the 2 mile handicap. He held his own all through the race although his opponents, who paced each other in turn, did their utmost to come up to him. He made a grand finish nearly half a lap in front of the nearest man to him and received quite an ovation from the assembled throng. He won his heat in the same grand style. The value of his prize was £6.6s"

In 1899 reporting on the Town's Sports of 19th August, the Dursley Gazette lamented the non appearance of some racing cyclists. "Mellerup, who had intended turning out on the celebrated Pedersen machine, was one of these, he having sustained injury in a smash up at Radstock (Sports) only a few days previous."

Racing at sports days was usually under the rules of the National Cyclists' Union and in May 1898 'The Pedersen Cycle Club', with distinctive racing vests, was formed and, one assumes, affiliated to the Union.

In July a Grand Military Tournament was held in Dursley to raise money for the Dursley Volunteer Rifle Brigade. It began with a colourful procession which included members of three cycling clubs — Dursley, Berkeley and Pedersen. "The Pedersen machines were ridden A.A. Lister, Mellerup, Jorgensen and Rasmusser".

A month before the Dursley Gazette stated:—

"A well known Dunlop Professional cyclist and holder of several records, named Green, has lately been on a visit to Dursley trying the Pedersen bicycle, which by the way is gradually gaining headway in the wheeling world thereby causing a demand on the resources of the local manufacturary. The other day the rider 'went for' Whiteway which he ascended with comparative ease. Mr.

MR. A. E. MELLERUP PUTS THE PEDERSEN
THROUGH ITS PACES

Anders Mellerup racing, about 1898
(R.A. Lister & Co. Ltd collection)

Pedersen is the only other cyclist who has mounted this steep incline on a bicycle.''

Harry Goss Green, one of the great cyclists of the day, used a Pedersen on 14th November 1898 to break the London to Brighton and back unpaced road record, recording a time of 6 hours 8 mins. 11 secs. 15 min. 14 secs. faster than the previous record. The Pedersen he rode, weighing 16 lbs and having a 100 inch gear went on show at the National Cycle Show that same month.

1898 was not without its tribulations. In April fire broke out in the "residence of Mr. M. Pedersen, the well known inventor and manufacturer. Many of the inhabitants of the town were aroused from their 'first nap' about half past eleven by the clanging of the fire bell over the Town Hall and the streets were soon alive with persons enquiring the cause of the alarm. The outbreak, it appears, was caused by the bursting of a lamp in one of the bedrooms at a time when no one was in the room .....'' Helpers managed to stamp out the fire before the fire brigade galloped down Long Street to the blaze but not before £50 worth of damage had been done to bedding and furniture.

The fire however was not the greatest trial of the year.

In June 1898 E.T. Hooley was declared bankrupt. In his bankruptcy statement Hooley made allegations of corruption against directors of such companies as Dunlop, Humber, Raleigh, Schweppes, Bovril and the Cycle Manufacturers Tube Co. and the resulting outcry and examinations filled columns in the Dursley Gazette.

Hooley's departure must have shaken the Pedersen Frame Co. Ltd. but Mikael, undismayed, continued to develop cycles. At the beginning of 1899, a ladies bicycle "with dropped frame suitable for riding with ordinary skirts" was seen locally; a machine forecast in the cycle patent of 1893.

However the loss of Hooley as a backer, coupled with the apparently less than enthusiastic production of Pedersen cycles by other companies must have led to some hard thinking about the future of the machine and the Frame Company, for on 8th July 1899 The Dursley Gazette announced "that arrangements are now being made to develop the manufacture of the Pedersen bicycle ....We believe that it only requires the introduction of good commercial methods into its manufacture and to be placed prominently before the public to ensure a large sale.''

That 'good commercial management' came with the entry of the Lister Family.

Chapter Two
The Dursley Pedersen Cycle Co.
1899-1905

"A Gloucestershire firm are said to have acquired a patent for the manufacture of a 12lbs bicycle which will carry a 14 stone man. One thousand machines are being made and they will soon be on the market."

The Gloucestershire firm was the Dursley Pedersen Cycle Co., the town name being added to Pedersen presumably to distinguish the firm set up in the Summer of 1899 from other Pedersen cycle makers. The owners, Robert Ashton Lister, his son Charles and Mikael Pedersen received license from the Pedersen Cycle Frame Co. Ltd. to make cycles in November, and in return agreed to pay the Frame Company 5s. (25p) royalty per cycle on a fixed basis as follows:—

Year ending 1st May	Royalties on
1900	250 cycles
1901	2000 cycles
1902	3000 cycles
1903	4000 cycles
and so on until	
1909 and onwards	10000 cycles per year

Optimism for sales was high!

Frames were to be numbered in order of manufacture.

Until this time Pedersen cycles made in Dursley bore a "Mikael Pedersen" head badge if they had one at all. Now a new badge was designed and registered as a trade mark, the badge which is now

A unique ladies' 'Mikael Pedersen' cycle. It was made by Mikael for his wife, Dagmar, and later given by her to Mrs. Adams, a friend, who is seen with it here. (C. Adams)

The same ladies' cycle in 1973 (R.F. George)

Head badges. Left: 'Mikael Pedersen' up to mid 1899
Right: 'Dursley Pedersen' post 1899.

commonly associated with Pedersen cycles.

For the new Company Mikael invented and patented a new front forks head, with ball instead of plain bearings, and made provision for adjustable handlebars. At this time too he produced a cycling costume for ladies "unrivalled for elegance, comfort and appearance which may be described as a most clever combination of the skirt and the pantaloons. Made in blue or black serge, with white facings, this is the ideal garb for lady cyclists."

By 1900 the Water Street works were well tooled and quantity production was under way. In that year the firm became incorporated as a 'limited company' with Pedersen, Robert Ashton and Charles Lister as Directors.For three years the company seems to have run smoothly, the Listers supplying the business acumen, A.E. Mellerup in charge of actual productions and Mikael free to develop and invent.

The Boer War was in progress and he turned his attention to this. At the end of March 1900, the Dursley Gazette reported that "the inventive genius of Mr. M. Pedersen has broken out in a new direction" with the production of "the handiest military bicycle yet made." This was quickly followed by a new design of gun and rifle carrier. Of all these 'The Field' in June gave an account. "For the sake of lightness and portability the experimental machine was built with a low frame and 24ins. wheels, the seat being fixed farther back than usual. By a very simple device the frame can be disconnected (from the front forks) at the head in a few seconds for the purpose of carriage. Instead of attaching the rifle rigidly to the machine as is customary, it is carried in a vertical position in front on two light projecting arms which work against a spring, so that it is a live instead of a dead weight. It can be detached in a moment and fired without dismounting, the lowness of the seat enabling the rider to rest both feet on the ground. The ammunition is carried in a bandolier, the mess tin behind the right shoulder and the rolled overcoat lower down. The bayonet is strapped on the left breast with the scabbard projecting over the shoulder. When the bicycle has to be carried it is disconnected and the front wheel with forks and, handlebar, secured by the side of the other by a single strap. It is then hoisted over the left shoulder where one pedal, dropping over the point of the bayonet, gives it good purchase. The arrangement leaves the right arm free for using the rifle .... The bicycle Mr. Pedersen has built to illustrate these devices weighs between 15lbs and 16lbs only but for ordinary purposes he would make the weight to about 19lbs.

"With the full load weighing close upon 35lbs., exclusive of the

Ride "Dursley Pedersen" Cycle

**Adjustable Saddle
and
Handle-bars.**

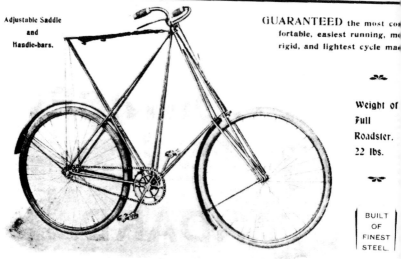

GUARANTEED the most comfortable, easiest running, most rigid, and lightest cycle made.

Weight of
Full
Roadster.
22 lbs.

BUILT
OF
FINEST
STEEL.

IMPORTANT TO MEMBERS OF C.T.C.

We will send a "Dursley Pedersen" "on trial" to any member of the C.T.C. furnishing satisfactory references. The "Dursley Pedersen" is sold on its merits.

Prices and full particulars sent post free by Sole Makers :

The
"Dursley Pedersen"
Cycle Co., . . .

 DURSLEY, . . .
GLOUCESTERSHIRE.

"Dursley Pedersen"
Ladies' 1900 Model

A Revelation to Lady Cyclists for Comfort, Lightness, and Rigidity.

A 1900 advertisement

Dursley Pedersen Cycle Company, Limited.

INCORPORATED UNDER THE COMPANIES ACTS 1862 TO 1890

SHARE CAPITAL £20,000

In 5,000 Preference Shares and 15,000 Ordinary Shares of £1 each.

Ordinary Share Certificate.

REGISTERED OFFICES: **DURSLEY PEDERSEN WORKS, DURSLEY.**

This is to Certify that *Mikael Pedersen*

of *Raglan House Dursley*

is the Registered Proprietor of *One Thousand* Ordinary Shares of £1 each

fully paid Numbered *7301 to 8300 inclusive* exclusive in

the DURSLEY PEDERSEN CYCLE COMPANY LIMITED, *subject to the Memorandum and*

Articles of Association of the said Company.

Given under the Common Seal of the said Company

the *ninth* day of *February* 19 01

W. R. Ashworth SECRETARY.

DIRECTORS.

N.B.—No transfer of these shares can be registered without the production of this Certificate.

Dursley Pedersen Cycle Co. Ld.

Mikael's certificate for 1000 shares in the Dursley Pedersen Cycle Co. Ltd. 1901
(Gloucestershire Records Office)

bicycle, Mr. Pedersen in order to discover the capabilities of the machine, rode from London to Dursley, 112 miles on one of the hottest days of last week and covered the first 102 miles in 11 hours 45 mins ...."

Mikael's interest in the army was more than passing. On at least two occasions widely spaced he was actively involved. Perhaps it was the excitement and physical excercise that appealed to him. The first occasion known happened in May 1901.

"Many of our readers will be interested to learn that Mr. Pedersen of Dursley, who has been doing useful Scouting work with the Yeomanry during camp at Badminton, was by invitation from Lord Roberts .... enabled to exhibit his ingenious feather weight bicycle and military outfit to (this) great authority on military matters. The Commander-in-Chief expressed himself very pleased with what he saw and appeared impressed with the service-ableness of the equipment. His Lordship commented most favourably upon the improved bandolier .... The saddlery was made to Mr. Pedersen's instructions by Mr. W.H. Fox of Dursley."

Spurred on by the praise, Mikael patented a few months later ideas on ammunition receptacles in bandoliers on belts, a military luggage carrier and further improvements to his gun carrier.

Alas, the army was interested in all the effort — but that was all. The Danish Army was the same. The story is told of how Pedersen having made a quick firing gun, tried to sell it to the British War Office. Objection after objection was lodged, each demolished by Pedersen until at last he was told that it could not be used by the army as ammunition could not be made quickly enough! This may be mythical but has the hallmarks of truth; Pedersen's ingenuity and the fate of many of his inventions!

On the civilian front, Pedersen cycles were getting around.

"Goss" Green of Silverdale C.C. set about breaking more road records in 1900. In turn fell the London to Portsmouth and back; in August — London to Liverpool; in October — London to York and World's 100 mile and 12 hour records, the last three in one glorious ride during which an "auxiliary hand driving mechanism" was used. Green's results are summarised below:

Event	Previous record	Beaten by Green, unpaced by
London to Portsmouth and back, 139 miles	8hrs. 36 mins.	23 mins

London to Liverpool 203 miles	11 hrs. 43 mins *paced*	43 mins
Worlds 100 mile	5hr. 4 min.	23 mins
London to York 197½ miles	12hrs. 6mins. *motor paced*	1hr. 47mins
World 12 hour	201 miles	24 miles

F.T. Bidlake commenting on the London to York run said it was thrilling to see Goss Green fly down Spittlegate Hill into Grantham "pedalling really fast on a gear of over 90, on a brakeless featherweight, and with the rocking mechanism of the auxiliary hand gear in a condition of rapid activity!"

Tourists took Pedersen cycles abroad. In February 1901 the company proudly announced that they were "executing a special order ... for the personal use of His Majesty the Sultan of Morocco. This order is the result of a recommendation by an English Tourist." One can't help speculating on the effect the arrival of this had on the Sultan's harem!

In those first years the works and staff expanded and sales grew. In the year ending 31st August 1900, £5015 worth were sold; in 1901, £7596; 1902, £10,418. In this year in response to demand, a new 'low' price model was produced at £18.18s. (£18.90), roughly £5 cheaper than the only gentlemen's model of previous years.

The cycle works became a place to visit. Early in 1902, a delegation from "The Implement and Machinery Review" toured the Lister Companies and in the cycle works were duly impressed when "taking a front fork which is regarded as the weakest part of a 'safety' it was placed on the ground at an angle by Mr. Pedersen, who with one of his assistants upon his back, stood on it (and) it sustained no injury."

In July of the same year at the invitation of R.A. Lister the Gloucestershire Chamber of Commerce came to Dursley and saw his churn and cream separator works and the cycle works. They too

Mikael ready for battle. The cycle is probably the military model, with his own design of gun carrier, and the bandolier probably his patent version (Toke & Vagn Jensen)

GENTLEMEN'S ROAD & PATH RACER

As ridden by Harry Green.

GENTLEMEN'S A1 MODEL ROADSTER.

14

A page from the 1905 catalogue

were impressed "Everybody cycles now-a-days and thus the process by which the iron steed is prepared for the yearly increasing demand was one which all the visitors watched with the closest attention."

At about the same time the Rev. Sidney Swan provided some excellent advertising. As a young man he had excelled in many sports including running, rowing and cycling. In 1902 when aged about 40 years he left his Carlisle Parish for a long ride and without any special preparation rode to London. Shap Fell was climbed in pouring rain, he punctured at Lancaster, he was cut and bruised when knocked off his cycle by a dog near Towcester, yet the distance of 301 miles was covered in less than 24 hours. His Pedersen weighed 25lbs and had a single gear of 80 inches. A remarkable performance.

Mikael Pedersen meanwhile, rebuffed by the army, thought of new ideas. At the end of 1902 came a patent for a new way of tinning cast iron and in the following January a patent for an internal combustion engine. For this was developed a motor cycle frame — Pedersen style.

Mikael's interest in motor-cycles seems to have come from his association with 'Humpage, Jacques and Pedersen'. This Bristol firm, in which he had invested money, made engineering news in 1898 when it produced novel drilling machines, one of which, described as 'sensitive', would drill or countersink in the ends of round or square section metal rod. At about this time several British inventors were designing engines for motor cycles, a field up to that period largely dominated by European engineers. One such was John Joseph Barter who lived in Luckwell Lane, Bristol close to the works of Humpage, Jacques and Pedersen. In about 1902, it was arranged that H.J. & P. should make and market 'Joe' Barter's engine — single cylinder with unusual features — under license. This was done but few machines were sold and the venture failed. Barter then developed a twin cylinder model 'The Fairy' which was taken over in 1907 by the Douglas Company of Kingswood. This may account for Mikael's choice of a Douglas in later years.

More important, however, was the birth of his variable gear hub, important both from the point of view of the significance of the invention itself and because it marked an unhappy turning point in the relationship between Mikael with the Lister family. It is ironic that a brilliant invention which could have brought him a fortune, brought instead much bitterness.

There had been several previous attempts to produce a variable

Advertisement of 1904. On the right is the Rev. Sidney Swann.
(R.A. Lister & Co. Ltd collection)

Anders Mellerup on a Pedersen motor cycle, about 1903
(R.A. Lister & Co. Ltd collection)

gear for cyclists but none really successful. The breakthrough came in 1903 when two 3 speed models came on the market, the 'Sturmey-Archer' and the 'Pedersen'. Which inventor can claim precedence is a matter of doubt.

Early in 1902 the Raleigh Company set up a department to improve and perfect an invention of Alfred Pellant and Henry Sturmey and by July they had succeeded. Pedersen had by this time spent some years on his device which he patented in August 1902. What is clear is that the principles behind the two gears are so different that there is no question of copying. The Pedersen gear was the simpler and stronger of the two and worked on the counter shaft principle; the Sturmey Archer gear was epicyclic.

By March 1903 the Pedersen gear was ready for the public and Mikael planned with Messrs Truscott and Son Ltd., "makers and sellers of bicycles" in Stroud to make and market them. However, R.A. Lister got wind of this and in June protested that the invention belonged to the Pedersen Company. Reluctantly, it would seem, Mikael accepted this and agreements were signed granting the company sole rights to make and sell the gear providing sales were pushed hard.

Mikael received £750, royalties of 7s 6d (37½p) per gear and the guarantee that the name 'Pedersen Hub' would be stamped on every mechanism. In return he promised to give his services in superintending manufacture and designing tools. By this time however, late 1903, Mikael had a business relationship with the Wolseley Sheep Shearing Co. Ltd. in Birmingham to whom he had sold a cream separator invention (in spite of the fact that it would compete with the 'Alexandra' and 'Melotte' separators of Listers both of which he helped to develop!) As a consequence an order for the first 1000 sets of gear parts had already been ordered (September) from Birmingham.

As parts arrived in Dursley they were assembled into complete gear hub units and sold but immediately there came complaints from customers of slipping — the friction clutch was not strong enough. Mikael, ignoring the advice of Anders Mellerup for a toothed clutch, and the only one who could make alterations under the agreement with the Pedersen Company, travelled constantly between Dursley and Birmingham, as did much correspondence, making modification after modification. For six months there was little result except a growing exasperation between the Pedersen and Wolseley companies, until in July 1904 the problem was partially solved. By this time the Wolseley Company had completed the contract and had a great pile of tools made useless by the

The Dursley Pedersen Cycle Co. work force. Seated in the front row (7th & 8th from left) are W.J. Ashworth and A.E. Mellerup. Taken about 1904 by the Raglan House cycle track. (B. Ashworth, Cam.)

MILITARY
AND
FOLDING
MODELS.

18

age from the 1905 cycle catalogue

W.J. Ashworth, Commercial Manager of the Cycle Works, in 1900
(B.J. Ashworth)

frequent changes in design made by "your Mr. Pedersen."

Although Summer 1904 brought in a crop of praising testimonials for the gear, there is no doubt that the friction clutch continued to make a basically very sound invention, unreliable.

One casualty of the situation was Mr. W. Truscott who in return for 2½% commission guaranteed to sell 1000 Pedersen cycles and 5000 gears in 1904. In advertising the gear and arranging wholesale delivery he lost £500 and plaintively wrote in February 1905 to Charles Lister that "he was in hot water all over the country for non delivery of the gear".

By February 1905 the Water Street works had some 28,000 parts awaiting assembly, a thousand or more useless friction clutches and a book full of orders they were unable to meet.

The Pedersen Company's reputation must have suffered, sales fell, and by the end of 1904 it had a deficit of £3000.

In January 1905 the Directors met and decided to sell. A month later the company was wound up and its assets and liabilities taken over by R.A. Lister & Co. Ltd. On February 10th cycle production entered its fourth phase.

Frame of a Pedersen motor cycle
(D.E. Evans 1974)

Chapter Three
Proprietors R.A. Lister & Co. Ltd. 1905-1917

As soon as the cycle company was fully under the control of Listers the friction clutch of the variable gear was replaced by positive toothed drive and immediately a reliable mechanism resulted.

At this point one must feel great sympathy for Mikael Pedersen. Two great brainchilds of his life, his cycle and his variable gear, were no longer his to do as he pleased with. Life must have seemed empty after the tremendous activity of the preceeding months — all Mikael could do was to await royalties and perhaps brood.

It is clear from documents of the time that R.A. Lister too felt sympathy for this brilliant but stubborn man and made great allowances for his unpredictable behaviour.

William Truscott of Stroud has been mentioned before. With new owners in charge of the Water Street works he again offered to promote the gear, this time by attempting to get other manufacturers to make it under license. In this he had some success as in June he notified R.A. and Charles Lister that the John Marston and the Premier Companies were interested. Mikael was informed and said he would consider the matter. A few days later while R.A. Lister was abroad promoting the gear, Mikael revoked the agreements of 1903, giving as his reason that Listers had failed to push sales of the gear. For Listers this was a blow as special staff at high wages had been taken on to make the gears. They continued to produce the gear however having no difficulty in showing that the reverse of Mikael's charge was true as the following list of advertising material for the 1905 season indicates.

1.   The printing of 37,725 gear catalogues.
2.   The printing of 17,927 general catalogues which included a section on the gears.
3.   Advertising by numerous show cards, leaflets and spaces taken up in trade papers, C.T.C. Gazette etc.

In October Mikael threatened legal action but suddenly in late

over of the 1905 cycle catalogue. The boy's 'paper' pulled out to give basic
formation and prices.
..A. Lister & Co. Ltd collection)

Advertising in the U.S.A. by R.A. Lister & Co. Ltd. — the back of a blotting pad.
(Toke & Vagn Jensen)

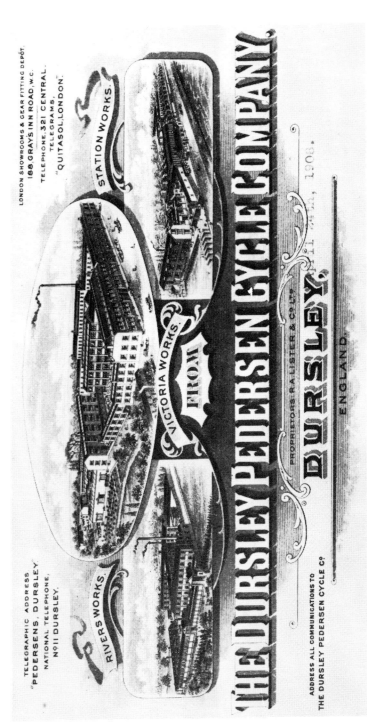

Company note paper heading after 1905. None of the scenes, all of which show considerable artistic licence, depict the cycle works.
(R.A. Lister & Co. Ltd collection)

November and early December a flurry of letters and telegrams resulted in the case being settled out of Court. In return for £1000, royalties of 7s. 6d (37½p) per gear, fourteen manufacturing machines from the cycle and separator works — his invention, and the freedom to develop other variable gears, Mikael agreed to allow Listers to continue making the gear.

From now on Mikael Pedersen seems to have had little to do with the cycle works where for several years sales increased reaching a record level of £22,841 in 1908 for cycles and gears. Thereafter figures fell slowly until 1914.

Very little advertising was done locally, in fact only one advertisement has been found in the Dursley Gazette for the whole 20 or so years of the cycle's manufacture. This was in the Spring of 1906. Listers however must have been conscious of the local townsfolk as in 1907 the great attractions at the July Fete was to be a 'draw' for "a Dursley Pedersen cantilever cycle fitted with Pedersen 3 speed gear, value £15.15s. (£15.75p)" Admission tickets, 1s (5p) each, or 6d (2½p) if bought before hand, would be used for the draw.

On July 27th the Dursley Gazette devoted 12 column inches of small print to reporting the draw. A churn was lent by R.A. Lister and after much coaxing a small girl from the crowd picked the winning number. It was held by Sgt. Fussell the "popular conductor of the Uley P.S.A. (Pleasant Sunday Afternoon) Band." So popular was he that the reception he got from the great throng made him too overcome to speak!

At the end of 1907 "Kuklos" the cycling correspondent of the Daily Mail recounted his experiences with a 3 speed Pedersen gear fitted to his honeymooning Chater Lea tandem. The Pedersen works supplied him a slightly modified version "but with 2 pairs of eight inch cranks and 2 fairly strong riders driving them, we put all the pinions in the hub to quite as severe stresses as they are ever likely to have to face and they all came unscathed out of their exceptional ordeal."

From 1904 a 2 speed gear had been made but this was discontinued in 1908. It was in the year that Listers decided to take up the manufacture of power driven sheep shearing equipment. ".....we had not only the machine tools in the cycle department .... but also the personnel capable of being trained ...." Anders Mellerup left the cycle side to take charge of the new department and production started.

Mikael's ingenuity was by now waning. He continued to invent in his workshops at Raglan House but all his patents relate to

One of Mikael's developments — a wheel cutter. 1908
(Toke & Vagn Jensen)

improvements to established items.

By 1907 he had produced a new cream separator for the Wolseley Sheep Shear Co. of Birmingham which was marketed from 1908 as the 'Wolseley-Pedersen Separator' for many years. Then came:—

February 1909	An improved cartridge belt
October 1909	Improvements to centrifugal cream separators
December 1910	More improvements to cream separators
Summer 1913	
and	
January 1914	Improvements to variable speed gearing

In August 1913 the Dursley Gazette reported:—

"It has been common knowledge for some time that Mr. Mikael Pedersen of Raglan House ... was busily engaged in the production of a new three speed gear and free engine clutch for motor cycles and our readers will be pleased to know that the result of a stern test made in the presence of several experts last Wednesday, was entirely satisfactory.

"Representatives of Motor Cycling papers attended at Birdlip Hill near Cheltenham where such trials usually take place. Mr. Pedersen rode a 2¾ h.p. Douglas motor cycle of standard pattern with side car containing 3 persons (his family) in order that the appliance might be subjected to a very stern test.

"He was able to get up the long steep hill easily at a high rate of speed, much faster than that of an 8 h.p. cycle car containing three persons which went up at the same time. The speedometer on the car registered 15 miles an hour and Mr. Pedersen's speed was estimated at about 20 miles an hour.

"The new gear which is very high, is chain driven and saves rubber tyres absolutely from wear caused by the uneven pull from the engine."

Further comment indicates that the gear was virtually the same as the 3 speed cycle gear — perhaps more robust.

The magazine "The Motor Cycle" devoted a whole page to the gear under the title "The Pedersen — Alpass Three Speed Hub Gear" and ended by stating that the Pedersen — Alpass firm hoped to be making the gear in quantities within six months.

For a while Mikael probably felt that his star was in the ascendant again but it was not so. The motor cycle gear came to nought. Delay in perfecting the cycle gear had lost to that, its deserved popularity; the motor cycle gear had the same fate — it was too late. The story might had been different if he had

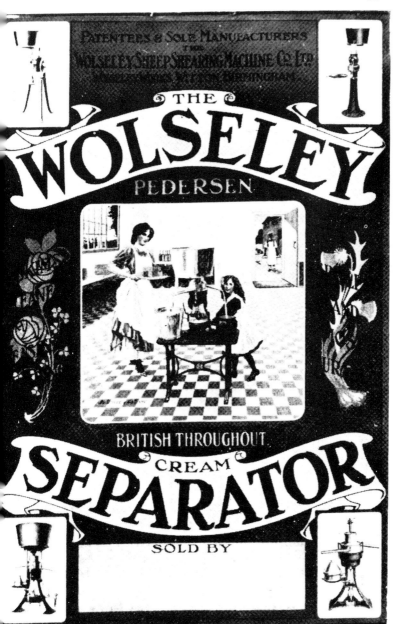

909 Wolseley-Pedersen Cream Separator show card. Down the sides are the omments 'Skims cleaner, easiest running' and 'Simplest and most durable' Museum of English Rural Life, Reading)

Mikael, family in the wicker side car, proves his motor cycle gear on Birdlip Hill near Cheltenham in 1913. ('Motor Cycle')

Pedersen-Alpass motor cycle gear in situ. 1913 ('Motor Cycle')

developed its potentialities as a counter shaft gear box mechanism instead of sticking to the hub gear already becoming obsolescent for motor cycles.

It is not certain who Mr. Alpass was but it is likely to have been one of the family who for some years at the beginning of the century ran a cycle shop and furnishing stores in Parsonage Street, Dursley, (where "Fine Fare" now operates). The family was go ahead. They were one of the first firms to use photography in newspaper advertising and a picture in 1904 shows their interest in the rapidly expanding motor trade. In 1905 the shop sold Dursley Pedersen cycles at discount prices.

Production by Listers of Pedersen cycles and gears continued at a slowly declining rate until the summer of 1914 when on the outbreak of The First World War all cycle parts were transferred to the garage of Mr. Timbrell in Cam. The garage still exists just to the south of Draycott Mills. The Water Street works turned to the production of items associated with army firearms. Advertising stopped at this time but sales of cycles and probably some assembling continued until 1917. Then on the advice of A.E. Mellerup who could see no future for the cycle, The Dursley Pedersen Cycle Co. (Proprietors R.A. Lister) ceased to be.

The end of the Dursley Pedersen Co. was however not the end of the Pedersen Cycle. In February 1921 it was announced in the C.T.C. Gazette that the entire stock of cycles, fittings and 3 speed gear parts had been taken over by the "Pedersen Cycle Company" of 24 Danes Road, Forest Gate, London. Another firm on the scene was the "Stephenson Cantilever Cycle Co." of Holloway, also in London. This firm advertised cycles made by "late Dursley Pedersen mechanics" between 1920 and 1922.

How long each of these firms continued with Pedersen design machines is unknown — probably only a few years. The world after the war was very different to that before. The Edwardian age of elegance and of wealthy leisure in which Mikael's bicycles had found a niche had gone. Tastes changed too. Even by 1910 a writer could comment "Wherever I go with (my Pedersen cycle) the youngsters hail it with the same remark 'What a funny bike'."

A proud owner of a post 1905 cycle
(R.A. Lister & Co. Ltd collection)

Chapter Four
Pedersen Gauges Ltd.

At the beginning of the First World War Mikael Pedersen enlisted in the patriotic but unofficial "Dursley Civilian Force", later the Volunteer Training Corp.

In early 1916 a new company was formed — "Pedersen Gauges Ltd."

"This Company has just been registered with a capital of £3000 .... to adopt an agreement between Mikael Pedersen and Ferdinand Kohn to carry on the business of manufacturers of and dealing in gauges, gauge screwing and cutting machinery, and tools and castings used in connection therewith, explosives for naval, military mining, engineering or other purposes, shells, projectiles, bombs, small arms ammunition, naval and military equipment and stores etc."

So far as is known only thread gauges were produced by this new company which operated in workshops at the back of Raglan House and also upstairs in the house in what had been a music room. The rough work was done downstairs and the finishing processes in the house, some by girls.

Castings for the gauges were made in Bristol. Mikael at this time was not an early riser and Mr. B.S. Webb, then a young lad fresh from school remembers having to pelt down Long Street on more than one occasion to the railway station to ask the Station Master to 'hold the train for Mr. Pedersen'.

The gauges when finished were tested at the National Physical Laboratory at Teddington.

Work at the tiny factory was sometimes late in starting. Many of the machines were operated by an engine run on town gas and when local housewives were over active, gas pressure was insufficient to get the engine going.

An interesting story seems to come from this period. Mikael was approached, it is said, by the British Admiralty and asked if he

The Pedersen Gauge Company work force in the grounds of Raglan House 1916.
Back row: Mikael and Ingeborg, Mr. Faija, Frank Owen, George Barnett,
Arthur Hollingsworth, Mr. Tegetmeier, Bella Cross, Wally Moore.
Front row: Mr. B.S. Webb, Edgar Letcher, Toke and Vagn, Gladys Shipton,
Lucrecia Trollope.
(L. Balman)

could devise a way of separating oil from boiler water for the country's steam powered warships, on the lines of a centrifugal cream separator. He was given a warship in which to conduct experiments but before these were complete, the Admiralty decided to change to oil engined vessels.

To begin with sales of gauges were high and the company flourished but towards the end of the war it found itself in financial difficulties. As the company operated in Raglan House this was caught up in these problems.

Early in 1918 Mikael thought of transferring the gauge works to 'Stroud Metal Works' at Dudbridge on the outskirts of Stroud. This came to naught as did another idea — that of making use of Coombe Mill, just outside Wotton-under-Edge, which Ingeborg, Mikael's third wife had bought sometime before. In the event, the Gauge Company closed and Mikael and Ingeborg moved to London in April. Their three children, all boys, went to stay in the Forest of Dean near Cinderford with "Aunty Gertie", a former maid in the Pedersen household who became a friend to Ingeborg. Later they too went to London. The connections with Dursley were now at an end.

The three sons of Mikael and Ingeborg, about 1918 — Toke, Sven and Vagn.
(L. Balman)

Chapter Five
Pedersen's Cycle

Although described at the time as a cantilever machine, technically this is a misnomer but it made interesting and catchy advertising as did the slogan 'Made like the Forth Bridge."

The triangulation gave good fore and aft rigidity but those prone to put great pressure on the pedals criticised the sideways 'give' in the bottom bracket area — one reason perhaps why it was not popular with racing men — except for a while with "Goss" Green, but then it was said that he could break records on a wheelbarrow.

Another criticism of the first cycles was the lack of adjustability: Beyond screwing or unscrewing the nipples on the spoke like rear tension wires to alter the sag of the saddle slightly, there was none. This was overcome for the early models of the Dursley Pedersen Cycle Co. in 1899 by using telescopic tubing at the rear so that the back end of the saddle could be raised or lowered several inches, and by introducing, as mentioned before, adjustable 'top of apex' handlebars. Apart from allowing adjustment of the bars there may have been another reason for this upward shift in handlebar attachment position — apprehension.

Said F.T. Bidlake in the C.T.C. Gazette of October 1897 in reviewing the Pedersen Cycle "the tubes ..... converge to a point ..... so high as to cure (the rider) of any nose-on-handlebar proclivities, and even suggest that he might be spitted thereon in case of accident. You sit astride a Clifton Bridge and face a pier."

As has been stated, the framework of the earliest machines was largely of wood, probably hickory. Some reports say that the wooden parts were bound by fisherman's twine, other say pinned, to metal joints. Perhaps both methods were used as prototypes developed. Whatever the construction, these first machines were rugged and carried their inventor over thousands of miles of rough roads.

a fact which can be demonstrated by putting the two ends of the fork to rest on supports (bridge wise) and placing heavy weights on the centre of the fork where the crown plate is fixed, care being taken that

the weight is resting on the crown plate, from whence it is distributed to the tubes as shown above.

A demonstration of the strength of the front forks — 1906 catalogue. The crest at the top of the page was commonly used after 1905.

Writing in the 1903 edition of the Boys Own Paper, the Rev. J. Hunt, an acquaintance of Mikael, states that he, Mikael, once spent £100 on building a real "featherweight" machine from the lightest tubes available which "cost twice as much as though they were made of silver." The tubing came from Accles & Pollock, Birmingham, it is said, as indeed, it seems did all the tubing used, and the castings for the joints were made in Dursley.

This remarkable machine still exists, rescued from the scrap heap in the 1920's by a former employee of Listers, Mr. E.K. Benjamin. Brakeless and tubular tyred it weighs approximately 9lbs. This lightness was obtained by reducing components in size to the minimum. The 30 gauge tubing can be deformed with pressure between finger and thumb, the 24in wooded rimmed wheels have wire spokes cleverly fitted straight into hubs to avoid any bending, and the wheel hubs, sprocket, wheel nuts, axles, and pedals are drilled out and cut away to an incredible extent. It is almost unbelievable that such a fragile machine could support a man but doubtless it supported Mr. Pedersen!

Another model just 11lbs was ridden to London from Dursley in 1904 and exhibited at the Stanley Show.

The weights of multiseat machines are given as:

Tandem	28lbs and able to support	24 stone
Triplet	45lbs and able to support	36 stone
Quadruplet	64lbs and able to support	?

These super light machines were exceptional and signs of the inventor's exuberance. The more usual size for tubing was 20 to 24 gauge, ½" diameter mainly but wider for the chain stays. In 1900 the original pattern was advertised at 20lbs, the adjustable 2lbs heavier. As the years passed however weights increased to over 30lbs in 1906 and later still 35lbs.

★

The prices of early Dursley Pedersens are recorded as between £20 and £25. In 1902 when the Gents Royal model retailed at £23.10s. (£23.50) a cheaper species, the Model 'A', was introduced at £18.18s. (£18.90).

By 1905 prices had dropped to £16.16s. (£16.80) for the Royal and £13.13s. (£13.65) for the Model 'A' and stayed at roughly these values until production ceased. Ladies models sometimes cost a little more and the inclusion of a 3 speed gear raised prices by £2.2s. (£2.10).

From time to time other models were introduced and also a number of optional extras. The table below gives dates of some

Super-light weight racing cycle with wire spokes and wooden rims, about 1898
(R.A. Lister & Co. Ltd collection)

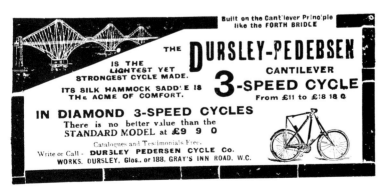

'Built … like the Forth Bridge' — an advertisement from about 1910

introductions but is not intended to be exhaustive or definitive.

The Dursley Pedersen Cycle Co. 1899-1900; *Ltd.* 1900-1905

1900   Ladies, Gents Original, Gents adjustable, freewheel, back pedalling hub brakes, rod rim brakes.

1901   Folding and Military cycle

1902   Cable brakes, ''anti-vibration'' handlebars. Cheaper Model A ladies and gent's machines.

1903   3 speed gear with friction clutch and handlebar control.

1904   2 speed gear (friction clutch), racing cycle, front and rear luggage carriers golf bag and gun carriers.

The Dursley Pedersen Cycle Co. Ltd. (prop R.A. Lister & Co.) 1905-1917

1905   The golf bag and gun carrier and racing and folding cycles were discontinued. The 2 and 3 speed gear were changed to toothed drive.

    Diamond frame machines were introduced at £8.17s.6d. (£8.87½) with single free wheel. These were not made on the premises but bought elsewhere. 'Star', 'Hopper' and 'Dingley' seem to have been sources.

1907   Anti-tampering device for gears.

    Diamond frame ''Road Racer'' at £9. Racing 'cantilever' cycle reintroduced at £11.15s. (£11.75)

1908   2 speed gear withdrawn

    Frame bag at 10s.6d. (52½p)

1909   Anti-rust model with aluminium pedals and wheel rims and handlebars covered in celluloid at £15.15s. (£15.75) with 3 speed gear. By this year cheaper 'cantilever' and diamond framed machines were in existence.

The 1911 catalogue lists the following cycles and these were continued until at least 1914.

Adjustable 'cantilever' with 3 speed gear:—

	Gents	*Ladies*
Royal	18 gns	18 gns
'A'	15 gns	15 gns
Standard	11 gns	£12.3s.6d.
Anti-rust	15 gns	

Diamond frame with 3 speed gear:—

Royal	11 gns	£12
Standard	9 gns	£10.5s.

The original 'cowhorn' pattern handlebar cycle was not often advertised in catalogues after 1905 but some were made, at least from time to time up to the First World War. The 1914 catalogue advertises this model at £12.12s.6d. with 3 speed gear and

ÐERSEN
RRIERS

PEDERSEN
GOLF
CARRIER.

For
Price
see
page 19.

ge from the 1905 catalogue.   Note the Doctor's bag on the carrier.

GENTLEMEN'S "MODEL ROYAL"

SPECIFICATION & PRICES

FINISH—Beautifully Nickel Plated and Polished on Burnished Copper throughout; or if preferred Enamelled in Green, Black, Claret, or other Colour.

FRAME—Dursley Pedersen, Built with Finest Quality Weldless Steel Tubing, specially selected for plating.

SIZES—	Nos. 1	2, 3, 4,	5, 6, 7, 8,
Suitable for an inside leg measure, fork to ground (fitted with 6½in. cranks) of	Ins.—27½	29, 30, 31½	33, 34, 35, to 3
WHEELS—Front and Back	Ins.—24	26	28
TYRES—Dunlop ...	Ins.—1½	1½	1½
CRANKS—Special Design	Ins.—6½	6½ or 7	7 or 7½

GEAR CASE—Carter-Pedersen detachable oil bath (if required and if extra weight not objected to).

GEAR—70in. or to order

PEDALS—Extra Quality Rat Trap, Felt or Rubber

FREE WHEELS AND BRAKES—If only one Gear is required this Bicycle is fitted with either a Combined Free Wheel Hub and Two Hand Rim Brakes, or with a Back Pedalling Coaster Hub. All Bicycles with variable gears are fitted with the Pedersen Two Hand Rim Brakes. Back Pedalling Rim Brakes can be fitted in combination with variable gear, (except when Gear Case is fitted) at an extra cost of 15/- nett.

MUDGUARDS—Detachable Plated Steel

HANDLEBAR AND SADDLE—Dursley Pedersen, Adjustable, Extra Finish

HANDLES—Finest Quality, White Felt, Cork or Celluloid

EQUIPMENT—Tool Bag, Spanners, Pump and Clips.

Prices as above, with Free Wheel and Two Hand Brakes		**£16 16**
,, as above, with Pedersen Two Speed Gear ...		**17 17**
,, as above, with Pedersen Three Speed Gear ...		**18 18**
BACK PEDAL RIM BRAKE to Variable Geared Bicycles ...		**15/-**

Specification for the Gentleman's Model Royal' — 1906 catalogue. The 'Model A' was 2lbs heavier and there was less choice of colour and in fittings.

GENTLEMEN'S "MODEL ROYAL"

Weight without Free Wheel and Extra Brake from 23 lbs. according to size

  ,,   With Back Rim Brake and Free Wheel   ... $1\frac{1}{4}$ lb. extra

  ,,   ,,   Combined Free Wheel and Back Pedalling
          Brake   ...   . $1\frac{3}{4}$ lb. ,,

  ,,   ,,   Pedersen 3-Speed Gear and Free Wheel ... $\frac{3}{4}$ lb. ,,

  ,,   Equipment   ...   . $1\frac{1}{4}$ lb. ,,

  ,,   Metal Detachable Oil Bath Gear Case used instead of
       Celluloid Chain Guard   ...   . $1\frac{1}{2}$ lb. ,,

LADIES' "DIAMOND ROYAL'
SPECIFICATION.

FRAMES—Best Weldless Steel Tubing. Ladies' 20," 22," 24."

WHEELS—28"

TYRES—Dunlop or other high grade.

SPOKES—Rustless.

BRAKES—Revolving Lever or Inverted Lever.

GEAR CASE.—Pedersen, Metal.

RIMS—Black Centres, Red or Green Line outside

LINING—In 2 Colours

SADDLE—National (Brookes license).

STEERING LOCK.

TOOL BAG—Pedersen.

GEARS—Three-Speed Pedersen

Price—Fitted with Pedersen 3-Speed Gear, **£11 5s**.

Fitted with Free Wheel and Single Gear, **£9 12s. 6d.**

If Celluloid Chain Cover fitted in lieu of Gear Case, 5/- less.

Specification for the Ladies' 'Diamond Royal' — 1906 catalogue

LADIES' "DIAMOND ROYAL"

These machines are elegant in design, and of high-class finish throughout : extremely easy running and comfortable Constructed of the best quality material and built by experienced workmen, their durability is guaranteed.

detachable handlebars "enabling riders to vary the type of handlebar if desired."By 'type' was meant degree of curvature as 3, 5, 7 and 8 inch heights were listed. For these machines Pedersen gears could be had, but Sturmey Archer and Armstrong gears were alternatives.

Post Dursley Era

In 1922 a Cantilever Cycle Co. advertisement shows a 3 speed model with unusual (racing?) handlebars selling at 12 gns.

All through the life of the Pedersen Works, prices of machines were high compared to other makes. Intending purchasers were wooed with many inducements — free trial rides, a tour of the works, easy payment terms, discount for cash and in early days, in return for suitable references, cycles would be sent to prospective buyers on a 'sale or return' basis.

★

The frame tubing, tinned all over to protect it, was soldered into phosphor bronze bottom bracket castings. In 1905, the Gloucestershire Engineering Society visited Listers works and saw among other departments, the cycle factory. "At the end of the engine room there is a powerful dynamo which generates the electricity for lighting the works and for driving the machinery in the cycle works some distance away, and to which the party were subsequently conducted. Here they found more to interest and instruct. The extensive shops are full of machines which are extremely complicated, but which work to perfection. All these machines have, we believe, been designed and manufactured by the firm, and give them advantages which are possessed by no other cycle makers. There is one machine, for example, which cuts, puts on a thread one end, and bevels out and engine-turns a large hub piece all at one operation, cutting it from the solid bar; and there are other machines which do work which is even more complicated.

In the upper stories of the works, workmen are busy putting the frames of bicycles together, polishing the steel parts ready for plating, and burnishing the parts which have been sent up from the plating room. This work throws off a quantity of very fine dust, and for their protection the workmen wear face-guards which give them the appearance of strange sea monsters. The frames of the Dursley — Pedersen machines, after being put together, are immersed in a bath of molten metal, which sweats the parts together and ensures rigidity and strength, and they are then sent down to the plating room, given first a coat of copper, and next nickel plated and burnished. As in the fitting shops everything is done exactly to scale."

Inside the cycle works, about 1907. Some 100 frames and 30 people are visible. (R.A. Lister & Co. Ltd collection)

The assembled cycles appeared in many standard colours. Some examples are given below

1905   Nickel plated or enamelled in black, green or claret

1910   Nickel plated or enamelled in green, black or chocolate

1911   Khaki and, 1912, French Grey were added to the colour range

"If speedmen realised the wonderful responsiveness ..... the Pedersen would soon be flitting in haste down the Bath and North Roads" said Kuklos in 1907 — colourful they would have been too!

★

Because of the limited amount of adjustment possible, cycles were made in 8 sizes for men related to leg length and it was important to have the right size otherwise riding could be very uncomfortable. Ladies frames came in 3 sizes, A, B and C but ladies legs were presumably unmentionable as leg length is not referred to. The 'A' size was equivalent to a 22 inch diamond frame cycle with 24 inch wheels and 6½ inch cranks. One wonders how many ladies bought the C model equivalent to a 25 inch diamond frame with 28 inch wheels!

Frame size	1	2	3	4	5	6	7	8
Inside leg length in inches	27½	29	30	31½	33	34	35	38

★

Saddles seem to have been at different times made of silk or whip cord and occasionally leather covered. It is said that they came in different widths. It is also said that they were woven by local women but whether at home or in the cycle works is not clear.

The saddle with its intimate contact with the human anatomy drew many comments. Some disliked its sway but some eulogised over it.

'The Field' in September 1899 devoted 16½ column inches of small print to the comfort. The writer had ridden 2500 miles on a 23 inch Alpha Framed Bantam with Pedersen saddle and found the saddle perfectly stable even when descending hills with legs on the handlebars (This was common practice among early cyclists. In Mikael Pedersen's Cycle Patent of 1893 he mentions that the shape of the handlebars was partly so to allow cyclists to use them "as a foot rest.")

The writer praised the "Perfect ventilation" and lack of "perineal pressure" — phrases often used thereafter by the Pedersen Company in advertising — as well as the absence of "distressing symptoms when riding up to 90 miles (as in) the recent

A class at Cam Hopton School about 1902. The position, the dress and the cycle indicate that the boy on the right had some status.
(R.A. Lister & Co. Ltd collection)

Gentlemen's
Saddle.

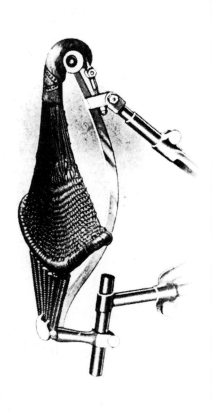

Lady
Saddle

16

Saddles for Gentlemen and Ladies — 1905 catalogue

Cover of 1911 catalogue (W. Bush collection)

Dursley-Pedersen Luggage Carriers
And Frame Bags

PRICES

Complete with Two
Straps.

PLATED.

Back ... 10/6
Front ... 8/-

ENAMELLED.

Back ... 8/-
Front ... 6/6

FRAME BAGS

Upper ... 7/9ea.
Lower ... 7/3ea.

1911 Pedersen luggage carriers.

tropical weather.''

★

The hub gear when first introduced must have been a wheel builder's nightmare. The pear shaped flanges required, it is said, twelve different lengths of spoke and although the company provided spoking charts they were not popular with wheel builders of other firms. A letter in October 1907 from W.J. Ashworth, then Commercial Manager of the Pedersen Works, to Mikael, states that manufacturers were "disgusted" with the trouble in building these hubs into wheels and were refusing to buy. By 1909 both flanges were circular.

The gear like the saddle had its converts. 'The Southampton Times and Hampshire Express' in 1904 extolled the virtues of the gear in a long article. After stressing these and explaining its principles it remarked "To alter the gear is extremely simple. It requires about as much exertion as is necessary in turning on the electric light and what could be more easy than that?''.

The gear gave a 50 % increase with each change upwards, which suited some people but not others. The gear tables opposite are representative. The 2 speed gears were 3 speed gears without the low range

★

Estimating the total number of Pedersen cycles made presents a problem. Anders Mellerup stated that some 30,000 were made (and 45,000 gears) but no frame number above 8000 has been recorded among cycles extant today (1978).

The memories of those who worked with the cycles, pictures, and known layout of the works, all support Mr. Mellerup. One theory to explain away the problem is to assume that the frame size number (the single digit or letter below the main number found on the bottom bracket) is also part of the numbering system employed.

Mr. G. Hall of Gloucester who has done much research into dating Dursley Pedersen cycles suggests the following:—

Main frame Number	Approx. date made
1 — 400	1900
400 — 1600	1901-03
1600 — 2250	1904
2250 — 4000	1905-07
4000 — 6000	1907-11
6000 — 7800	1911-14

'Mikael Pedersen' cycles can be dated to between early 1897 and mid 1899. A cycle with the Beeston badge is known and would date from the same period.

For 26 in. Back Wheel | For 28 in. Back Wheel

Number of Teeth on Bottom Bracket Wheel	Number of Teeth on Hub Chain Wheel				Number of Teeth on Hub Chain Wheel			
	9 x 1 or 18 x 1½		10 x 1 or 20 x 1½		9 x 1 or 18 x 1½		10 x 1 or 20 x 1½	
	Low	High	Low	High	Low	High	Low	High
20 or 40	58	87	52	78	62	93	56	84
21 42	61	91	54½	82	65	97	59	86
22 44	64	96	57	85	68	102	62	93
23 46	66	100	59½	89	71	106	65	97
24 48	69	103	62	93	75	112	68	102
25 50	73	109	65	97	78	117	70	105
26 52	75	112	67	100	81	121	73	107
27 54	78	117	69½	101	84	126	76	114
28 56	81	121	72	108	87	130	79	118

Number of Teeth on Bottom Bracket Wheel 1'' and 1½'' pitch	Number of Teeth on Hub Chain Wheel					
	8 x 1'' 16 x 1½''			9 x 1'' 18 x 1½'' 18 x 2''		
	Low	Medium	High	Low	Medium	High
20 or 40	47	70	105	42	62	93
21 42	49	73	109	43	65	97
22 44	52	77	115	45	68	102
23 46	53	80	120	47	71	106
24 48	56	81	126	50	75	112
25 50	58	87	130	52	78	117
26 52	61	91	136	54	81	121
27 54	63	94	141	56	84	126
28 56	66	98	147	58	87	130

⅝-INCH PITCH.

For 26in. Back Wheel | For 28in. Back Wheel

Number of Teeth on Bottom Bracket Wheel	Number of Teeth on Hub Chain Wheel			
	15 x ⅝'' pitch		15 x ⅝'' pitch	
	Low	High	Low	High
30	52	78	56	84
32	56	83	59	88
34	59	88	63	94
36	62	93	67	100
38	66	99	71	106
40	69	103	75	112
42	73	109	78	117
44	76	114	82	123
46	80	120	85	127

⅝-INCH PITCH.

Number of Teeth on Bottom Bracket Wheel	Number of Teeth on Hub Chain Wheel					
	13			15		
	Low	Medium	High	Low	Medium	High
30	43	64	96	38	56	84
32	46	69	103	40	59	88
34	49	73	109	42	63	94
36	52	77	115	45	67	100
38	55	82	123	48	71	106
40	58	86	129	50	75	112
42	60	90	135	52	78	117
44	63	94	141	55	82	123
46	66	99	148	57	85	127

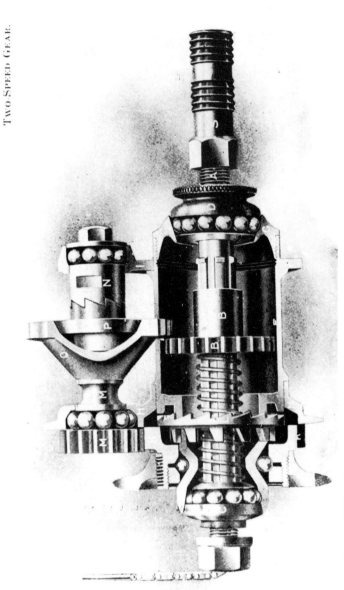

Two speed gear — 1905 catalogue

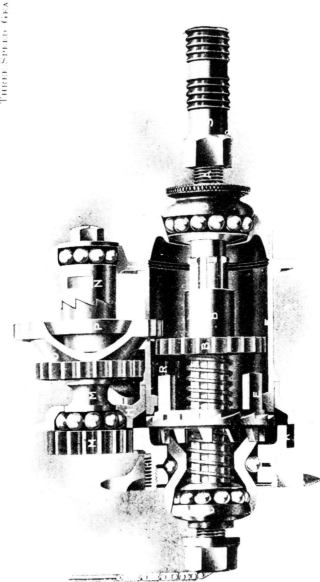

Three speed gear — 1905 catalogue

Three speed gear showing pear shape flanges of pre 1907 (B.J. Ashworth)

Three speed gear with circular flanges, post 1909 (C. Howarth)

According to local people who can remember the Pedersen works in later years, the firm employed some 40 to 50 people and turned out 20 to 30 cycles per week. The general opinion is that relatively few were sold locally, most being marketed through the London Depot —

1901-1905   College Hill Chambers, Cannon Street
1905 onwards   188 Grays Inn Road

Each cycle was crated separately and despatched from Dursley by rail. It is said that a high proportion found their way into the Eastern Counties.

Although annual sales in Gloucestershire seem to have been small over the years the numbers mounted up and many of these still exist as family heirlooms.

The children of the Lister family had Pedersen cycles and Arthur Hollingsworth remembers the youngsters on them swooping joyfully down the hill of Long Street. The messenger boys of R.A. Lister & Co. Ltd., also had Pedersen cycles until the cycle works closed.

★

The cycle as a whole was either loved or abominated, it couldn't be ignored. The Cycle Company made great use of the praise it got and its advertising, was full of good testimonials. If these are all to be believed — and why not? — the cycle had remarkable use and an equally remarkable clientele.

Here are some examples:—

1900   *'Bristol'* Lady rides from Bath to London 108 miles in 13½ hours, including 3½ hours of stops.

1902   *'Jersey'* Man rides 1020 miles at 70 miles a day over French rough pavement, cobbles and mountain passes without problems.

1910   *'Ringwood'* 12,000 miles ridden with only punctures.
            'Toft Manor' 60,000 miles ridden in 5 or 6 years.
            'Indian Army, Cheltenham' 10 years of very hard usage.
            'Royal Societies Club, London' 5 week tour in the Alps with 17lbs to 25lbs luggage.

1911   16 stone 'agent' carried 2000 miles.

By 1904 the firm could boast that Dursley Pedersen cycles had been bought by The Sultan of Morocco, the cricketing Prince Rankitsinjhi, the Marquis of Anglesey, 4 Admirals, 10 Army Officers from Captain to General, 8 Reverends, 8 Doctors, 11 assorted, notable gentlemen as well as many lesser mortals. It is probable that most of these 'well up in society' people transferred their attentions quite rapidly to the new motor car but some cyclists

am'. George Oram Warmer was a dispensing chemist in Berkeley, Glos., from
and, as well, was an active member of the Plymouth Brethren whose chapel
wo miles away. No doubt his 'Pedersen' served him well with both these
ests. (V. Rees)

Dr. E. Cyriax riding in London at about the age of 75 years. Taken in about 1949. ('Cycling')

continued to use Pedersen cycles long after the Pedersen Company closed.

T.H. Pettifer had at various times 3 models of Pedersen and rode one until two years before his death in 1954 at the age of 83 years. His tours included Switzerland, Austria, Italy and Spain and his cycle carried not only himself and general luggage but also stereoscopic camera and tripod.

A.W. Rumney was another Pedersen tourist and he visited France and Corsica, Italy and Sicily, Portugal, Spain, Greece, Algeria and the Middle East with baggage and camera. He found the Pedersen the best for rough roads for he had "ridden to Jericho over a kind of stone quarry" on one!

Dr. Edgar Cyriax, eminent consultant physician of London who died in 1956 aged 82 years, was a great believer in cycling for good health and enjoyment. In his life time he covered ¼ million miles, reaching as far as The Arctic Circle and Russia, much of it on a Pedersen.

Such great Pedersen riders linking us with the days of Mikael are no longer with us but for many the machine retains its charm and gives pleasure.

The whereabouts of some 100 machines are known to George Hall. Some are inanimate museum specimens but many enjoy an active life still. Their owners may belong to one of the Veteran Cycle Clubs which cater for people interested in old bicycles and their history. Such Clubs or Societies have active rallies and runs. One of significance was organised in 1973 by Bob George, then Club Captain of the Southern Veteran-Cycle Club. This was a two day ride on Pedersen cycles from Westminster Abbey to Dursley during the weekend 3rd and 4th March, and went by way of Newbury, Swindon and Tetbury. A great reception by townsfolk and members of staff of R.A. Lister & Co.Ltd. awaited the 10 or so riders as they descended the last hill from the top of the Cotswolds late on the cold Sunday afternoon.

If the shade of Mikael Pedersen was about then he probably smiled, remembering back 80 years, for that last hill was Whiteway.

LONDON -
DURSLEY (GLOS.)

3 - 4TH. MARCH 1973

BY MEMBERS OF THE SOUTHERN

VETERAN - CYCLE CLUB

ON

DURSLEY - PEDERSEN CYCLES

PROGRAMME & ROUTE

London to Dursley by Pedersen Cycle, March 1973. Programme cover.

London to Dursley ride 1973 — a stop at the top of Whiteway Hill above Dursley. Roger Armstrong, David Hibberd, Heywood Hill, John Bass, David Twitchett, Roger Pearson, Bob George — organiser, Marion James (J.P. Sirett)

London to Dursley ride 1973 — reception at the bottom of Long Street, Dursley.

Chapter Six
Mikael

"Some people to whom (Mikael Pedersen) showed (his cycle) in Birmingham regarded the experiment with distinct levity. One very much dressed individual had the delicacy to say 'none but a fool would ride a thing like that! Later on, on becoming impressed with Mr. Pedersen's evident knowledge of what he was talking about, that being a rather uncommon thing in Birmingham, this tasteful person inquired if he might try it. 'No' replied Pedersen 'I did not make it for fools to try' and the wind whistled through the keyhole like a woman in aguish.''

What was Mikael Pedersen like? Those who knew him, now have to cast their minds back sixty or more years but it seemed worthy trying to find out and here I must record the great pleasure I have had in talking to many of our local senior citizens.

Mikael was a musician. His music room in Raglan House contained many instruments some of which he had altered from standard or constructed himself. Among these were a French Horn with special mouth piece and bass and double bass viols on which he could get notes of uncommon difficulty. An example of Mikael's composition exists — a short, rather lilting tune that one might whistle when pottering on a cycle through country lanes. It is entitled 'Double Bass Dreams or Violin Whims'. As written it goes up far beyond the normal range for a double bass player yet a footnote on the score states that it should be played even higher — two octaves higher! Some of his own wind and string instruments were not very successful but a few were later improved and found their way into the band of R.A. Lister & Co.

Like many a genius, Mikael was often lost in thought. Heeding no one, striding, black bushy bearded, perhaps in Norfolk Suit, through the town, he was something of a frightening character to children and even some adults.

He was a gentle, generous man who inspired great respect, even

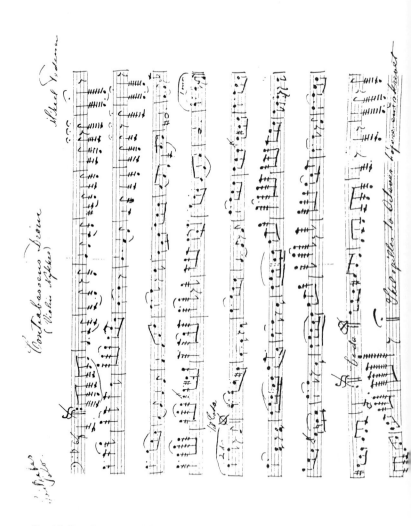

'Double Bass Dream or Violin Whims' — a composition by Mikael Pedersen
(Toke & Vagn Jensen)

affection in his workmen. To some, to have worked with Mikael was a marvellous, unforgettable experience. He talked easily and in good English to his employees and on one occasion at least, during the First World War, gave them a party in which he was very jolly.

Mikael's ideas tumbled out of him to such a degree that employees were sometimes not allowed to finish one job before being put to another. Foundry moulds left over night were sometimes found to be cut with a pen knife in the morning, ideas having come to him in the night. He was a stubborn man, very obstinate when he had an idea. He could generally produce what was wanted but he was no business man.

Being Danish, Mikael obviously hoped that some notice of his cycle would be taken in Denmark but in this he had little success. His application for a patent there in 1897 was rejected on the grounds that it was too complicated.

On another occasion he tried to interest the Danish Army in his military cycle. He rode from the family home in Marjberg to Copenhagen but finding that he was late, left the cycle at a grocers shop on the outskirts and continued by train. The interview was probably a stormy one for at its end, his idea rejected, Mikael in great anger returned straight way to England, leaving his cycle unclaimed.

Mikael was a demanding man in affection. He married but failed to have children and so, as he was then able to under Danish Law, he divorced his first wife, Laura, and remarried. Dagmar, his second wife also bore him no children and he was joined in England by his third wife, Ingeborg, in 1906. Ingeborg gave him four children, Margarethe who died in 1910 after only a few months of life, Toke, Vagn and Sven. For one of his sons, Mikael built a miniature bicycle for use on the Raglan House cycle track. Maybe Mikael joined his son occasionally by riding one of the several 'ordinaries' or 'penny farthings' he kept in the stables.

The family had little contact with the townsfolk in later years Mikael didn't seem to need the company and the local people regarded them, foreigners at this time before travel was widely indulged in, as rather strange beings. They were not, however, isolated. R.A. Lister visited them at Raglan House and Mikael sometimes visited the homes of his employees and doubtless there were other contacts.

Mikael's second wife, Dagmar, joined him in cycling and they were often seen out together. Dagmar is said to have posed for early Pedersen advertisements. The last recorded ride of Mikael was in 1908 when one January evening he was stopped by P.C. Iles

Mikael, his third wife Ingeborg and two of their children. Possibly about 1913.
(Toke & Vagn Jensen)

in Kingshill Road for failing to have lamps lit, his new acetylene lamp having let him down. Thereafter he seems to have turned to walking.

During the war Ingeborg worked in the munitions factory in Dursley. After she and Mikael moved to London in 1918 relationships between them strained to breaking point and in September 1919 Ingeborg left for Denmark taking the three children.

At about this time Mikael had an operation for cancer of one eyebrow. He was by now about 65 years of age and he seems to have exhausted his ambition and drive. He followed Ingeborg back to Denmark but rarely saw her or the children. In England he left all his property and finances to his second wife, Dagmar, who had remained in the country. Thus he arrived in his native land in about 1920 destitute, and for several years he stayed with some of his brothers and sisters, moving from one to another, just accepting his new life, bearing no grudges to anyone for past failures, nor bitterness for what might have been.

Much of this time was spent with Ole Hans Pedersen, his Lutheran Priest brother, and his family in the vicarage at Gemminge, near Randers, Jutland. Very generous, very kind, and a little boastful of his past and what he could do in the future if he tried, a great story teller, he sometimes greatly embarrassed Ole by revealing inside knowledge gained in the vicarage of village life.

By 1928 he was becoming too difficult for his relations to look after him and through the intervention of a friend — a former Danish Premier — he gained admission to "Den Gamle By" (The Old Town) Old Peoples' Home in Copenhagen. Here, aged nearly 74 years, on 22nd October 1929, he died.

★

How can one sum up Mikael Pedersen? A man often lost in thought or music, stubborn, erratic, sociable, brilliantly inventive, lovable and warm hearted, unable to understand the cold world of commerce, active and restless physically and mentally. Probably all these things — and certainly very much more.

★

In the introduction to this book I mentioned my visit to Denmark in the Autumn of 1977 when I stayed with Finn Wodschow. Together we pieced together the later years of Mikael's life and we visited Den Gamle By, the peaceful 'township' capable of accommodating over 1500 old people in pleasant rooms set round tree shaded squares, the last home of Mikael. The day after I left for England, Finn found the site of Mikael's unmarked grave in

Mikael and Dagmar Pedersen, about 1898. As Dagmar is riding a small man's cycle it is possible that she is wearing the divided skirt devised by Mikael.

Bispebjerg cemetary — Section 1, Row 43, Grave Number 41 — and placed on it a few flowers. It was a simple tribute from the two of us — and dare I say from all cyclists? — to a very remarkable man.

Appendix One

Some Major Dates

1855	Mikael Pedersen born near Copenhagen, Denmark, 25th October.
1885	Development of Pedersen Cream Separator.
1889	R.A. Lister acquired right to market the separator as 'The Alexandra'. First known visit of Pedersen to England.
1893	Probable year in which Pedersen settled in England. Cycle patent applied for in England.
1896	Pedersen joined Humpage, Jacques and Pedersen of Bristol. Pedersen Cycle Frame Company created. Water mill acquired in Dursley as a factory.
1897	Production of cycles began in Dursley. Other companies began to make cycles under licence. Pedersen moved into Raglan House.
1898	Tandem, triplet and quadruplet machines. Pedersen Cycle Club formed. Road record broken on a 'Pedersen'.
1899	Dursley Pedersen Cycle Company formed. Ladies drop frame cycle introduced. Ladies cycling costume introduced.
1900	Military folding cycle introduced. More road records broken.
1902	Pedersen motor cycle produced. 3 speed gear patented.
1903	3 speed gear produced.
1904	2 speed gear introduced.
1905	Pedersen Co. taken over by R.A. Lister and Co. Ltd.
1907	Wolseley-Pedersen Cream Separator developed.
1908	2 speed gear discontinued.
1913	Motor Cycle gear developed by Pedersen.
1914	Dursley Pedersen cycle production ceases.
1916	Pedersen Gauge Company set up in Raglan House, Dursley.
1917	Sales of Pedersen cycles by Listers in Dursley stops.
1918	Pedersen and his wife move to London.
1920-22	Pedersen cycles made and sold in London.
1920	Pedersen returned to Denmark.
1929	Mikael Pedersen died on the 22nd October.

Appendix Two

Mikael Pedersen's account of how he came to create his unusual cycle. It is taken from an early, undated catalogue, perhaps the first issued.

"I have been a cyclist for more than twenty years, and have done much hard riding, sometimes 5,000 miles in one season. I soon found there was much room for improvements in the construction of cycles, although it was only when I got my first "safety" that I saw how much yet remained to be done in this direction.

The part of the machine in general use which I found especially imperfect was the seat. There have, it is true, been many attempts to make better seats, but none were what I thought completely successful. I made several experiments before I could get exactly what I wanted, but finally my efforts were crowned with success. The seat which I have devised is, as you will observe, made of strings of different degrees of tension, running from a point in front to a cross steel bar giving the requisite width behind. In order to give the right width and form, cross strings are interwoven. The seat is suspended between two supporting points about two feet from each other; and running from the cross steel bar to the rear supporting point are several spiral springs, which afford the requisite elasticity. It will be seen that this seat (called by some the "hammock", and by others the "network" seat) can never become hard or too wide at any point, although it gives the rider more space than do other seats. As, moreover, it "gives" in every direction, the weight is always evenly distributed. You may take my word for it that all cyclists — and especially ladies — after once trying this seat will refuse to ride on any other. Its weight is not more than four ounces, as against the (about) 3lb. of an ordinary saddle.

Seeing that I should want so much room between the two points for suspending the seat, I found it almost impossible to make a new seat frame which would not be too heavy, and which would have an elegant appearance. I resolved to make a cycle frame which would carry the seat without the necessity of having a special seat frame at all. In the ordinary "safety" I found the frames were so far from perfection that I had to abandon that system entirely, with the exception of the two tubes running from the bottom bracket to the rear wheel spindle. Now, in order to have a strong support in front for the suspension of the seat, and at the same time to hold the top pivot for the front fork, I let one tube from each end of the bottom-bracket tube run to the supporting point, where they are joined. Two other tubes run from the supporting point to the rear

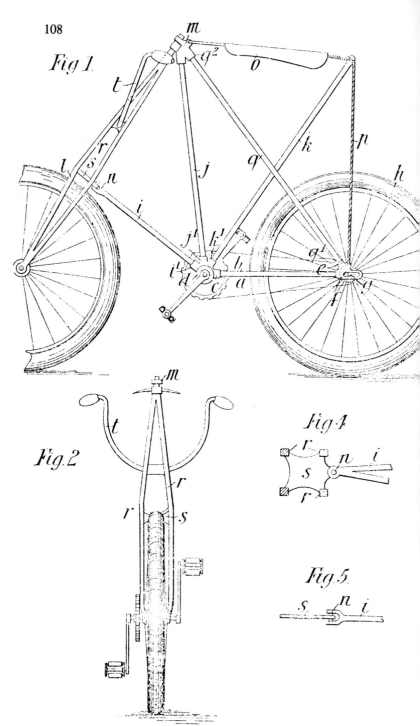

Diagram with the first British patent, Sept. 1893 (Gloucester Records Office)

ends of the hind wheel fork, forming two perfect triangles, joined at the top angle; where they carry the seat from the front fork pivot, and are held apart in the two other angles by the bottom-bracket barrel and spindle from the rear wheel. This is the real body of the frame, and the great strength of it will be easily understood.

To form a strong support behind, from which the seat is suspended to its support in front, I build another tube from each end of the bottom-bracket barrel running to the required point, where they are joined; and from there a wire runs down on either side, where they are connected to the rear ends of the hind wheel fork, forming two other perfect triangles, joined at the top, and held apart beneath in the same way as the above-mentioned triangles; the tubes running from the bottom bracket to the hind wheel spindle form the basis of the triangles in both cases. It will be seen that in no other way could equally strong supports for the suspension of the seat be made, unless at the sacrifice of lightness. Nothing like the common front fork could be fixed to this frame. I may say that I never approved of the manner in which these forks were built, inasmuch as they were weakest where they ought to be strongest, and heaviest where they ought to be lightest.

I build my front fork of four tubes, which I join at the top, where they carry a pivot spindle. About midway there is a crown plate, which carries the bearing for the pivot bolt, and keeps them apart, so that from there to the top the fork consists of four perfect triangles. On each side two tubes are joined at the lower end, thus forming a fork for the front wheel, each side consisting of a perfect triangle. Made in this way, the front fork is so strong that, although weighing only rather more than half a pound, it will carry a rider of sixteen stone over a rough road. To transmit the steering power to the front wheel the handle bar drops, to allow room for the knees, thus enabling the bar to be built into the strongest part of the forks connecting all four tubes. The pivot spindle at the top of the fork is fitted into the bearing at the top part of the frame from which the saddle is suspended. At this point the centre lines of all the eight tubes meet. To hold the front fork at the right distance below, a tube is built out from each end of the bottom bracket, the tubes running towards the middle of the front fork, where they are joined, and carry a seat for a pivot bolt, by which it is pivoted to the crown plate in the front fork. The bottom bracket barrel, which has to stand the heaviest strain of all parts of the frame, is, as I have shown, held by four tubes at each end; and this accounts for the immense strength of the frame.''

Appendix Three

Notes on Early Patents

Patent No. 18371 — Improvements in Bicycles

Applied for 30th September 1893 — Accepted 4th August 1894. This makes it clear that one reason for the 'cowhorn' style of the handlebars was to enable riders to use them as foot rests when descending hills.

The patent in the provisional specification describes a ladies drop frame, though this wasn't made until 1899.

Patent No. 16899 — Improvements in Bicycles

Applied for 30th July 1896 — Accepted 17th July 1897.

This relates to improvements in making joints and saddles. In the latter the side cords were left slack so that the saddle was able to 'accommodate' itself to the shape of the rider.

Patent No. 27769 — Improvements with Pedals

Applied for 25th November 1897 — Accepted 15th October 1898.

Important points were that:
  (i)   the ball races were such that pressure on the balls was vertical and not diagonal as with conventional cones.
  (ii) threads on pedal axle were of 'turret' type to give a firmer hold on the crank.

Patent No. 27771 — Improvements with Crank Axles and Bottom Bearings

Applied for 25th November 1897 — Accepted 15th October 1898.

In this, each chain wheel screwed onto its axle and bearings were such that pressure on the balls was vertical.

Patent No. 28485 — Improvements in Bicycles

Applied for 2nd December 1897 — Accepted 15th October 1898.

This was concerned with multi-seat machines — tandem, triplet etc., and advocated the use of bracing stays to strengthen the front forks and the main frame.

Patent No. 17185 — Improvements in Cycle Frames

Applied for 24th August 1899 — Accepted 28th July 1900.

The construction of a ladies drop frame, modes of constructing heads with plain or ball bearings and a way of making provision for ordinary handlebars, are all described.

Fig.1

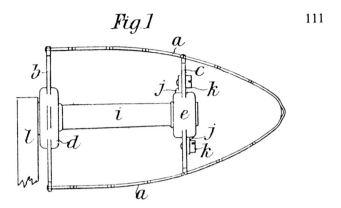

Fig.2

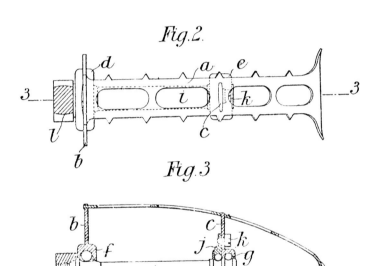

Fig.3

Fig.4

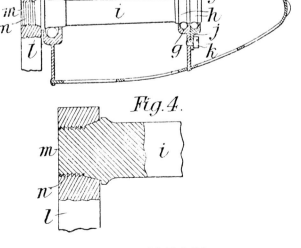

Patent 27769, Nov. 25th 1897 — pedals (G.R.O.)

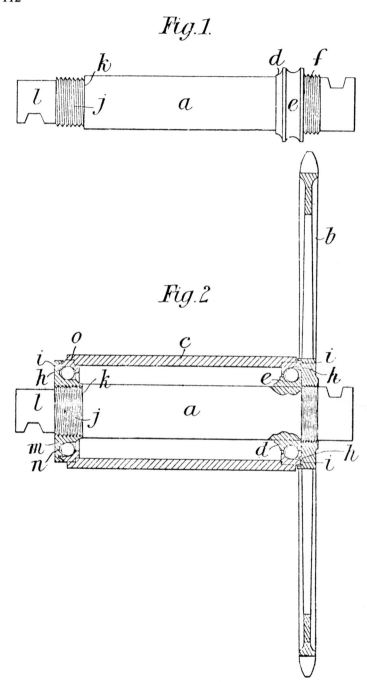

Fig.1.

Fig.2

Patent **27771** Nov. 25th 1897 — chainwheel and bottom bracket fixing (G.R.O.)

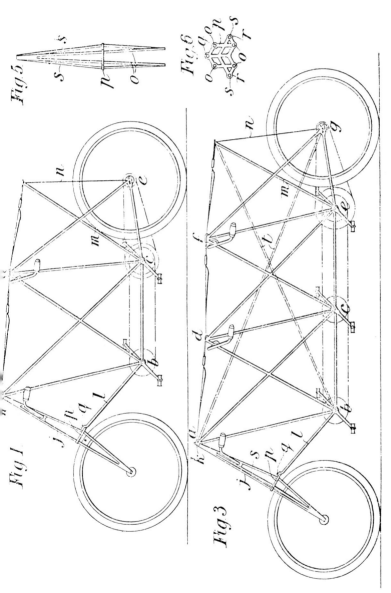

Fig.1

Fig.3

Fig.5

Fig.6

Patent 28485, Dec. 2nd 1897 — tandem and triplet (G.R.O.)

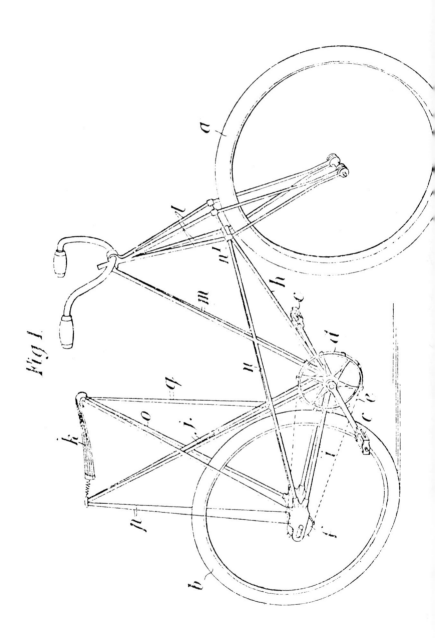

Fig 1.

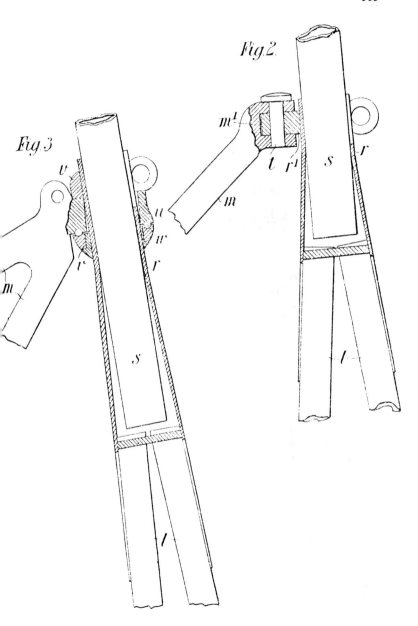

Patent 17815, Aug. 24th 1899 — Fig. 3, man's cycle with ball bearings
Fig 2, lady's cycle with plain bearings

Appendix Four

A year or so ago, Mrs. D. Pinkerton was called into H. Peace & Co. of Birmingham to sort out millions of inter World Wars period transfers. The badge shown above was among them. Local enquiries about 'The Dursley Cycle' have been fruitless.

According to the Dursley Gazette, at the end of 1907, one William Bendall, a wheel builder at the Pedersen Cycle Works, after receiving a travelling bag from his colleagues, left for New Zealand. In 1908 he was recorded as being in charge of the 'Arcadia Cycle Depot' there, and he stayed until at least 1916. After the First World War he seems to have returned to Dursley for a while, but by this time the Dursley Pedersen cycle was out of production. Did he attempt to continue the 'Dursley' name by creating his own badge, the one above?

Appendix Five

Dursley & District Road Club was formed in the Autumn of 1970, the most recent of a succession, which began in the early 1890s, of cycling clubs in this small country town. The present club combines the touring aspect the original C.T.C. affiliated 'Dursley Cycling Club' and the racing side of its co-existing 'Pedersen Cycle Club'.

The Road Club emblem is based on the Dursley Pedersen cycle head badge by permission of Messrs. R.A. Lister & Co. Ltd.

Appendix Six

This Appendix Six appears only in the third edition of *The Ingenious Mr. Pedersen* published in 1984. It is derived in part from the information contained in the booklet *More of the Ingenious Mr. Pedersen* published in September 1979 by David Evans and Finn Wodschow.

Mikael Pedersen

The start of the First World War brought trade with Germany to a halt, and it was no longer possible to import such important pieces of equipment as magnetos for aeroplanes and motor cars, and several types of engineering master gauge. Each of these products was vital for the British war effort and into both fields plunged Mikael Pedersen to produce replacements – for the latter, at the urgent request of the National Physical Laboratory (N.P.L.) at Teddington.

The company of Pedersen Gauges Ltd., set up in Raglan House in 1916 (IMP p.66), exploited the results of a period of successful experimentation on ways to make the master gauges – plain, plug and thread or screw – capable of measuring to the accuracy of 1/10,000 inch as required by N.P.L. Mr. Ernest Hollingsworth, who worked as a boy with Mikael at this time, remembers clearly much of his ingenuity and his ability to make use of things to hand in a simple, but highly efficient, way.

To cut the threads on the gauges, Mikael used short lengths of needle inserted in lathe tools. The needles were hardened and ground to the correct profile and used on lathes similar to those of watchmakers. N.P.L. supplied large scale, accurate, drawings of the desired thread contours and Mikael checked his by projecting their silhouettes onto the drawings using an episcope.

The process of hardening the gauges had to be done in the absence of air to prevent distortion. Mikael's method can be understood by referring to the diagram. The gauges were embedded in friable clay and heated over a fire in the brick lined pit he had dug in his garden. Draught for this was provided by connecting it to a water pipe on the side of Raglan House. When at the

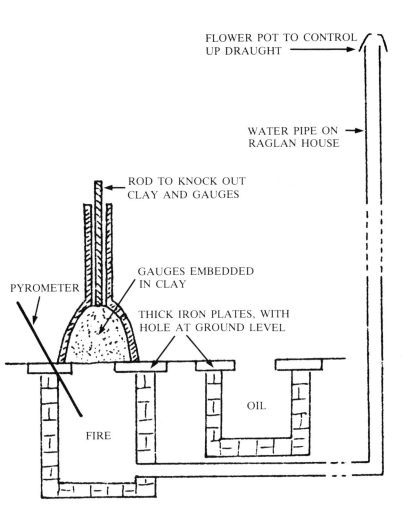

FLOWER POT TO CONTROL UP DRAUGHT

WATER PIPE ON RAGLAN HOUSE

ROD TO KNOCK OUT CLAY AND GAUGES

GAUGES EMBEDDED IN CLAY

PYROMETER

THICK IRON PLATES, WITH HOLE AT GROUND LEVEL

OIL

FIRE

120

Wheel Building at Pedersen Cycle Works c. 1910. Bert Ayland third from left. Others Left–Right: J. Williamson, S. Wakefield, (B.A.), W. Whittard

correct temperature the gauge holder was slid quickly over a bucket of oil, and the clay and gauges knocked in, the sudden, airless cooling gave the required hardening.

It is likely that the oil used was cotton seed since this was used in the nearby Lister's foundry. The workmen there discovered that it was also suitable for cooking. The Company, by means of the eagle eye of A.E. Mellerup, tried to prevent the movement of their oil into local chip pans, but had as little success as it had with the men in the cycle works, converted in the war into a small arms factory, who found that the brass rifle cartridge cases they were making were attractive as cases for cylindrical cigarette lighters!

The delicate lathes and grinding machines used by Mikael were bolted to the solid walls of Raglan House. They were belt driven from small electric motors by means of round boot laces and so steady that a glass of water, stood onto one while it ran, showed no signs of vibration.

Among Mikael's employees was Arthur Hollingsworth, pattern maker, elder brother of Ernest. One one occasion Arthur was set to dismantle a German magneto of the inverted 'U' type. Using the basic information thus revealed, Mikael then designed a simpler round model. His method of sketching out his ideas was unorthodox in that he superimposed all views, top through to bottom or side to side, to create one drawing. Part of Arthur's job was to disentangle these views.

Once invented, as so often happened, Mikael lost interest in the magneto. It was taken up by Charles Lister and mass production began in Coventry where it was marketed as the 'ML (Morrison—Lister) Magneto'. Most of the magnetos used in the war by the Royal Flying Corps, and industry in general, were of this make.

Thus in at least two ways, Mikael did work which was of vital importance to the country of his adoption in that difficult period. Probably his backers appreciated this, but financially it brought them little reward. The money they provided was used to develop ideas but Mikael rarely pursued them to the point of getting a return on the investment. They withdrew their support, one of the last being Mr. Alpass, auctioneer of Cam. Towards the end of the war Mikael was unable to pay his workmen and they left. The Government took over his machines and installed them in London where Arthur Hollingsworth spent six months training men to use them.

The Hollingsworth family lived at Hydegate Farm, Uley, having moved from London. Father was a blacksmith at Mawdsleys. His

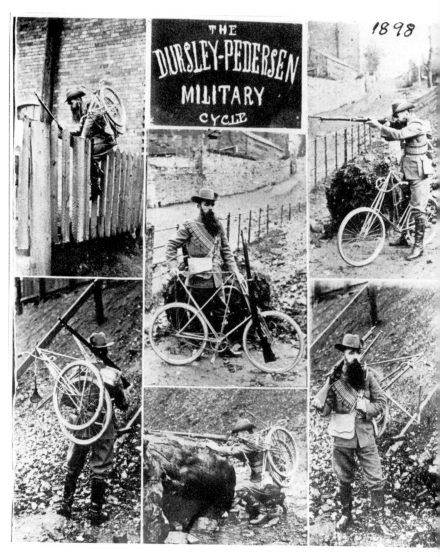

Mikael Pedersen and his military cycle — 1898? (Mrs. Baker)

eldest daughter, Ernest's sister, attended Miss Loxton's private school in Woodmancote. As she passed Raglan House daily, she collected Mikael's eldest son, Toke – a very inquisitive little boy – and took him to the same school.

During the war Mikael employed a Frenchman, James Devauden, as secretary. Devauden lived with an older man, an Austrian, Count Albrecht, up on the bank just beyond Uley's Fop Street cross roads. At first, the two were thought to be foreign spies by the locals and on one occasion, Boy Scouts were set to search the woods of the valley between the village and Dursley for incriminating evidence.

Mikael's enthusiasm knew no bounds. On one occasion he put considerable energy into inventing roller skates driven by body weight instead of the more normal thrusting action. Each skate incorporated a coarse screw. Foot pressure on this caused it to rotate the wheels – hence forward motion!

Mikael's generosity, evident at all times, was particularly obvious at Christmas. Water Street, where the cycle works stood, was lined at that time with small cottages, and the families that inhabited them were large – fourteen children was not uncommon.

Each Christmastide, Mikael walked the length of the street to give toys to the children – dolls to the girls, something mechanical to the boys – and a fowl or rabbit to the parents. For the latter Mikael set off on his cycle with his gun for a few hours shooting.

Wassailing was one of the Christmas activities of local workmen and Mikael and his wife Ingebord were as generous with food and drink as any of the occupants of the big houses of Long Street.

Such generosity however combined with lack of financial acumen brought the family to near penury at the end of the war. Mrs. Gwen Smith, once a maid at Raglan House, has vivid recollections of the shock and grief caused to the household servants when it was discovered one morning that the family had gone without warning.

Mikael was fond of a drop of beer and servants occasionally saw him come up from checking the wine cellar with froth on his whiskers. He was also fond of coffee – very well sugared – and Ernest Hollingsworth remembers that he carried an atmosphere, not of cigars, but of sweet coffee.

From time to time Mikael had twinges of rheumatism in his hands. To cure these he would send one of his workboys to find a number of bees – their stings he found to be an effective remedy.

Pedersen Cycles

One slogan used to advertise Dursley Pedersen cycles was 'Built like the Forth Bridge'. The idea of this may well have come from *The Captain – a Magazine for Boys and Old Boys*. In vol. VIII p.373, about January 1903, the cycling editor said of the Pedersen cycle:

'I well remember the startling effect of the first sight I had of one. It was leaning against the wall of a building at Whitminster, which is only a few miles from Dursley. It may, for all I know, have belonged to the maker, for the machines were not at that time on the market. I happened to be touring in that region, and at the first sight of what appeared to be a perfect monstrosity in cycle construction, I at once dismounted to examine it . . . One recommendation of all types of Pedersen machines is the splendidly strong design of what in other bicycles is called the fork crown. It always reminds me of certain lines in the structure of the Forth Bridge, and I should think that nothing but the most terrific impact would suffice to break it'.

Contact with the American student who acquired a Pedersen cycle in Exeter (IMP p.9) has been re-established. Chas. Wilson is now living in King of Prussia, Pennsylvania. His Pedersen cycle is believed to have been used by Lord William Gascoyne-Cecil, the 'Bicycling Bishop' of Exeter, 1916-1936, who was still cycling at 70 in 1933. In 1976 Chas. used the cycle for a remarkable ride in a day over the 100 miles from Philadelphia to Cape May. Referring to the saddle he commented afterwards 'On short trips it is incredibly comfortable but since it rises and falls with the rider, it sort of cuts off circulation after a while!'

The story that on one visit to Denmark, Mikael, his military cycle rejected by the Danish Army, left it in anger at a shop on the outskirts of Copenhagen is true (IMP p.101). Detective work has traced the grandson of the shop keeper and in the loft of his house is that cycle.

Mikael's attempts to patent his cycle in Denmark have also been discovered. These were in 1894, 1897 and 1898. All were rejected on the grounds that he was attempting to patent too much, though he was given 'exclusive rights'. He, therefore, applied for a patent for just the unique saddle and this was granted in January 1899. However, as the patent also included the frame for supporting the saddle, he achieved his aim!

A friend of Pedersen and A.E. Mellerup, whom Mikael brought from Denmark to be his chief engineer at the Dursley cycle works, was Gastav Wied, the well known Danish novelist. Wied, in his book *The Evil of Life*, combined the attributes of Pedersen and Mellerup to create the character of the customs officer, Knagstal. Mikael gave Wied a Pedersen cycle and the author willed that at his death it should be buried in his garden. So far as is known, it is still there.

A.E. Mellerup in the late 1890s was a member of the Bristol South Cycling Club. Probably his most famous exploit in cycling was to ride up Stinchcombe Hill via the very steep Hill Road and Broadway on a Pedersen cycle (IMP p.30). His first attempt was balked by a horse and cart blocking the way and he had to return to the bottom. On successfully completing the climb on the second attempt his pulse was checked by a doctor. Exhilerated by his achievement he went on to attack successfully the steep hills of Crawley and Lampern out of Uley, and Birdlip near Gloucester.

Acknowledgements

We acknowledge with great pleasure the help given with the above notes and pictures by:

Mrs. W. Baker, daughter of Anders Mellerup
Mr. & Mrs. D.H. Benjamin, Dursley
Mr. D.V. Fox, Dursley
Mrs. W. Gardner, Dursley
Mr. & Mrs. E.C. Hollingsworth, Hereford
Mr. C.E. Howarth, Uley
R.A. Lister & Co. Ltd.
Mrs. G. Smith, Dursley
Mr. Chas. Wilson, U.S.A.
and with the typing by:
Valerie Rodway, Cam.

References for the above

For IMP – read *The Ingenious Mr. Pedersen*

Above is Jesper Sølling with one of his cycles in the pose of author Gustav Wied.

Gustav Wied, 1910

The New Copenhagen Pedersen Cycle

Until recently Pedersen cycles in Denmark were almost unknown. Then a young blacksmith, Jesper Sølling, living with his family in a commune set up in a disused army barracks in Copenhagen, saw a book picture of one and made a crude repiica. From this chance beginning in 1978, and with the advice of cycle historian Finn Wodschow, a small but thriving Pedersen style cycle frame building business sprang into being. These Copenhagen Pedersen frames, made with modern techniques and capable of taking current standard cycle fittings, are exported to many parts of Europe. Such has been the number sold in the Copenhagen area itself that the 'Foreningen Pedersen' (Pedersen Association) was inaugurated in late 1982. The first cycle ride of this was a picnic run in May 1983 from Jesper's premises at 43 Badmandsstraede through the Danish capital to the Deer Park on its outskirts.

Commemoration of Mikael Pedersen's death

The fiftieth anniversary of Mikael's death was commemorated in Dursley in 1979. The event was organised with the active support of Messrs. R.A. Lister & Co. Ltd. in the person of the company's publicity officer, Don Asher. It drew a great number of Pedersen cycle owners to the town one Autumn weekend to take part in a tour of places associated with the Pedersen family and cycle making, a dinner at which his sons Toke and Vagn were present and honoured and a day ride through local countryside. The gathering reached its climax when the Danish Ambassador to Great Britain, His Excellency Jens Christensen, unveiled a plaque on Raglan House on 23 September in the presence of two of Mikael's sons. It was designed by Margaret Driver, art teacher at Rednock School, Dursley. The pattern maker was Bob Dix of R.A. Lister & Co. Ltd.

Pedersen weekend September 1979 — end of Sunday ride in Long Street
(Dursley Gazette)

Toke Jensen, Michael Lewis, Managing Director of R.A. Lister & Co. Ltd., the Danish Ambassador, Vagn Jensen and David Evans outside Raglan House on 23 September 1979.

Tailpiece

In 1904 a young lad, Percy Ashworth, began work at the firm of R.A. Lister & Co. Ltd. as an apprentice toolmaker. His father, W.J. Ashworth, has been mentioned before as being for some years Commercial Manager of the Pedersen Cycle Works and in those times young Percy must have met Mr. Pedersen on numerous occasions. It was an acquaintanceship that seems to have influenced Percy considerably, as it is said that he modelled himself on Mikael, and certainly when he grew to manhood he was restless, inventive and musical like the older man.

Percy was a life long member of the Cyclists' Touring Club, a member of the Camping Club and toured abroad as well as at home. He was responsible for several patents in industrial truck design and also patented a cycle gear by which riders pedalled backwards to climb steep hills.

At Listers he became a draughtsman and after reaching the age of 65 years was retired. This he never accepted and continued to work with the company until tragically in 1975, at the age of 88 years, he died after a collision with a fork lift truck.

In 1913 Percy Ashworth went for an Easter Cycling Tour on his Dursley Pedersen and for the interesting account taken from his diary, that follows I am greatly indebted to his son Mr. B. Ashworth of Churchdown. It is, I think, a good example, by a local man, of the extraordinary feats performed by cyclists at the beginning of this century on largely unsurfaced roads and shows how robust was the fragile looking Dursley Pedersen cycle.

Distance covered in two days approximately 140 miles.

Percy Ashworth outside his house in Uley, Glos, with a Pedersen cycle adapted to carry one of his children. About 1914. (B.J. Ashworth)

Over the
Black Mountains
with
Tent and Cycle

I started out from Gloucester at 7 a.m. on the 22nd March, 1913, having ridden up from Dursley the previous evening. The cycle, when ready for the road with the camping kit, weighed 70lbs, and the camera and food in a haversack which I carried on my back, another 10lbs.

The sky was veiled and a wind springing up from the S.E. presaged an approaching cyclone from the Atlantic. Taking the road west over the Severn I had a good view of the floods. I had a steady ride to Longhope and then commenced the ascent to Dursley Cross and was agreeably surprised to find that I could ride all the way up with no extraordinary exertion. Saw a lot of daffodils growing wild between there and Ross, which I reached at 8.45 a.m., having acquired a keen appetite for breakfast. After breakfast, forward again at 9.15 taking the Hereford road which crosses the Wye just below the town. The river was much swollen with flood water and was a turbid red colour and running at great speed. I turned to the left on the Abergavenny road some 3 miles or so from Ross and here it began to rain for the first time. I followed the road as far as Skenfrith on the Monnow. This river, like the others, was a rushing torrent, bank high and stained red with local soil. Here I stopped to photograph the falls and castle.

They have built a row of cottages up against the wall of the castle, thus saving one side of the houses. I turned north to Pontrilas here and expected a level road up the Monnow Valley, but they seem to have gone out of their way to take the road over every hill adjoining the river. Just before reaching Pontrilas I saw the road which I should leave it on, about 200 yards over the fields, but the river ran between and the road makes a detour of about two miles to this particular place. I caught the first glimpse of the mountains here and was surprised to see that they were snow covered. After Pontrilas I took the Abergavenny road which keeps close to the river and is consequently level. This I followed as far as

Llanvihangel Crucorney, where I got a fine view of Skirrid, with the clouds trailing across it. I immediately got out the camera and took the opportunity, which soon afterwards was gone, as the clouds then completely obscured it. I had now to leave the Abergavenny road and turn northward up the lane which leads into the Black Mountains. For the first 6 miles the gradient is about 1 in 15 and the surface passable. At this point the road crosses a bridge to the other side of the little river, which is its companion all the way up the valley. The place is called Llantony and there is a post office and an old abbey there. I stopped to post a card home but as it was still pouring with rain I did not stay to look at the Abbey. Soon after the road began to deteriorate and the gradient was frequently 1 in 4 and very soon it was not worth while mounting again. A few miles further on I passed a monastery. There was a high wall all round surmounted with several lines of barbed wire and pierced with one or two doors. A grave yard filled with tombstones and statues was adjoining, together with a few outhouses of the farm variety. I was anxious to get my camping site so I did not stop to see the monks. Past the monastery the road became a mere footpath and recrossed the river on a foot bridge, just above a fine waterfall. Just here I had to struggle up a 1 in 3 gradient covered with loose boulders and outcrops of rock. Then I passed through a gate on to the open mountainside. Leaning the cycle against the gate, I had a good look about for a site to pitch on. But there was no shelter from a possible sou'wester here so I pushed on through ever increasing snow drifts and pouring icy rain, along the barely discernable track. About a mile farther on I was surprised to see another cottage which proved to be the last in the valley. Half a mile past here the valley narrowed and perceiving a big hump of rock the other side of the stream I went down to investigate. After going up and down the bank for some distance in a vain search for a ford, I gave up the search and waded across. It was running at a tremendous rate and the bottom was covered with big boulders which were invisible in the red stained torrent. The temperature of the water was about 32 degrees, being melted snow. The site proved to be as good as I could expect up there, with good shelter from south to northwest, so I rewaded the torrent and unpacking the kit, threw most of it over and carried the rest. It now began to snow instead of rain so with all possible haste I scraped a patch clear of snow and erected the tent. I had considerable difficulty in tying some of the knots with my numbed fingers and to cap all the guy lines got tangled and it took some minutes to unravel them. I went inside and unrolled the ground sheet, taking therefrom my spare socks and trousers. Casting off my wet shoes, stockings and breeches, I put on the dry ones and as my overcoat had kept out most of the rain, I was then dry again. I filled the aluminium saucepan with water from a little lake just behind the tent and left the canvas bucket full outside the tent door.

I was soon having a well earned meal, bread and butter, buns, dutch cheese, cake and a quart of hot cocoa with plenty of sugar and condensed milk to keep up the body temperature. It was then 5 p.m. and I lounged on my blanket reading and toasting my feet at the Primus stove till 6.30 p.m. when I rolled myself up in the blanket and leaving the stove alight at my feet went to sleep.

After what seemed a short time I awoke and found it was 10.30. It was comparitively calm outside and all I could hear was the roaring of the torrent down below and the soft rustling, hissing sound of the snow falling on the tent. I refilled the stove with paraffin and wondered why the expected gale was not blowing. I afterwards read in the papers that that particular night there was a tremendous gale and some of the south coast piers and sea walls were destroyed. I put down my immunity to the splendid shelter I had from the big hump of rock. I woke again at 4 a.m. and found my blanket and clothes wet where I had been lying on them. I found out later that the adjacent lake had overflowed in the night and was pouring down under the ground sheet and out of the other end, over the bank and into the stream. Some of it had got over the top and consequently wetted me. I ought to have dug a slight trench round the tent on pitching it, but it was too much bother just then. I moved to the side of the tent where it was dry and dozed off till 5 o'clock when I got up and filled my saucepan from the canvas bucket outside the door. I opened a tin of sardines and ate half of them with bread and butter, and made another quart of cocoa. Immediately after breakfast I went out with the camera and climbed out of the valley up a steep snow slope of about 60 degrees angle. I stopped and looked down when near the top and it struck me that if I slipped I should go rolling and slipping to the bottom again, so I took considerable care afterwards to prevent anything of the sort happening. At the top of this steep slope the mountain rose at a moderate gradient for about half a mile and I plodded on to the top, generally up to my knees in the snow.

There was a stone hut just here with the door unlocked which I afterwards was told served as a base for the grouse shooting parties in the autumn. I went in, and shutting the door, changed the plates in my camera with the aid of my coat as a changing bag. This is an invaluable device when far from any dark room, as I was. I have done it a number of times now and had no appreciable fog on the negatives. There were a few sheep to be seen foraging for a meal on some of the bare patches and some birds I presumed to be grouse. It was now about 7 o'clock and the sun was rising, tingeing the clouds and snow with pink and orange, when I topped the ridge and came in sight of the Gaidair Mount. There are three main ridges to the Black Mountains and I was on the middle one. The eastern one was the other side of the valley from which I had ascended. The western one of which the Gaidair Mount is the summit (2660 feet) was partially hidden by the clouds and was completely snow covered. I had intended climbing the Gaidair but owing to the depth of the snow it would have taken 2 or 3 hours to have done it, so I regretfully left this for some future occasion. After taking sundry photographs of the sunrise and the cloud capped summits, I started the descent to the camp. It was nervous work going down the steep snow slope with the possibility of reaching your destination quicker than would have been comfortable. I reached the camp without mishap and started packing up again. An old Welshman came up just before I took the tent down and seemed very interested in affairs. He asked me if I went about camping all the year round and remarked that it was very nice to have plenty of money and go about where you liked. I explained that I had to work for my living, but had a few days holiday then, being Easter. He thought the camera was a surveying instrument, which was not a bad guess. He had a look inside the tent and noticing the candle holder hanging from the ridge, enquired if it was used to keep the tent down. As the sun was shining quite powerfully now, I took off my boots and stockings and spread them on a rock to dry. I walked about the snow barefoot, taking photographs of the waterfalls which afterwards proved to be failures owing to the plates not dropping properly. I then finished packing, and rewading the river I strapped the kit on the cycle. Putting on my partially dried shoes and stockings I started the arduous climb to the summit overlooking the Wye valley.

The road is very hard to follow from here to the summit and is frequently utilised by the numerous watercourses, so my stocking drying was of little use. The chief guide to the whereabouts of the road, was the fact, that as it was a slight hollow, the snow had drifted into it and left the exposed bank bare. If you want to know what hard work is, try pushing an 80lb cycle up a gradient of 1 in 4 through snow drifts. I had to 'rush' some of the drifts and back out again to renew the 'rushing' process till I got through. After a few minutes of this sort of thing one is apt to overlook the fact that the snow is cold. In one place the road coincides with the bed of the main watercourse which is only a fair sized brook up there. But it is very pebbly and filled with big boulders and a series of waterfalls, so I had to get my shoulder under the hammock saddle and carry the cycle through this particular bit. Soon after this the road attains the elevation of the tops of the main ridges and the valley peters out. Suddenly a wonderful panorama opened out ahead. I had reached the escarpment overlooking the Wye valley at Hay. All along this north side of the mountain the land drops suddenly at an angle of 45 degrees or so, down to the Wye which is but a few miles away. The top is probably 2200 feet above sea level and the Wye here is 300. Looking westward along the edge I could see Brecknock Beacon gleaming brilliantly in the sunshine, immaculate in its white covering. Far away in the north west was a fine snow capped ridge which I judged to be Plinlimmon, the source of the river which was winding its tortuous way down the valley beneath me. Again, in the N.N.W. and near the limit of sight, I could discern a fine range of snow mountains, which were probably the Arenig group. Never had I seen a more magnificent sight than what was spread out before me on that bright clear morning, and it was well worth the hard struggle I had had in attaining the top. After drinking it in for some time and expending my last two plates, I ventured over the brink, on the so-called road, hanging on to the caravan like a bulldog. After the first few yards the snow was drifted into the road hollow to a great depth. I probed with the tent pole in one place and could not bottom it, so it must have been 7 feet deep at least. Owing to the hardness and granularity of the snow, however, it was possible to get through without usually sinking above the knees, or the cycle above the hubs. In fact, I rather doubt the possibility of taking an 80lb kit down there, had there been no snow to hold it back. Half way down I had a rest, up to my waist in it and the cycle standing by itself. The wheels looked solid discs and the spaces between the lower frame tubes were filled up also. The drifts thinned out to nothing at about 1000 feet, as also did the road. I got out my map and pondered over it for some minutes and finally decided to go on down through the bracken to a farmhouse I saw in the distance. After fording sundry streams I reached the farm and found the termination of a rough lane. Following this down for a mile or two, sometimes riding, sometimes walking, I emerged into a fairly decent road leading from Talgarth to Hay on the Wye. On the road I took advantage of the improved surface, and ran down to Hay with a N.W. wind behind at a fine speed. I had a narrow shave in one place where the previous day's deluge had deposited a layer of brick red mud. I was rounding a long bend just here and the cycle was but a degree or so out of the perpendicular, but that was enough. It skidded on its original direction and saving myself from capsising by putting my foot down, I went bump into the grassy bank, broadside on. I did not even quit the saddle and pushing off from the bank, resumed my way. On reaching Hay I took the road to Ross via Dorstone and Peterchurch. This interposes a range of wooded hills between it and the Wye and rises for some miles. I took advantage of a heavy shower to shelter and dine at the same time, it being 1.30 p.m. Just here it is quiet pastoral country between lines of wooded hills. The hills run parallel to the Wye and each succeeding range is a bit higher than the previous till they culminate in the ridges of the Black Mountains of which the western ridge is the highest. Riding along here in the early afternoon with the sun pouring down on a hot white road, it looked quite incongruous to occasionally catch glimpses of the snow covered mountains. My stockings and shoes were quite dry now, being the first time since Saturday morning. All along through the Hereford lanes there was a profusion of primroses and white violets. The violets were as plentiful as the primroses and every now and again the scent would be wafted across the road. Near Tram Inn I was warned that the road was under water, but there was no convenient detour so I ploughed through it. It was about nine inches deep in one place and only by hard work I managed to keep going. I had just previously congratulated myself on being dry, but now my shoes were full of water again. I pushed on through undulating country, through Llanwarne, joining the Hereford - Ross road some few miles from Ross with the wind behind, at about the speed of the Gadarene swine.

My travel-stained appearance caused considerable interest in Ross and having passed all the police safely, took the road to Gloucester over May Hill. Here I caught up some motor-cyclists with side-cars who were evidently having trouble with the gradient, so I showed them the way to do it and we kept passing and re-passing each other all the way to the top, where of course I was left. Running down through Huntley I encountered all the folk on the way to church and looked as wicked as possible to shock them. The floods had subsided somewhat at Gloucester so I could take the short cut round Quay Street to Bristol Road. Plodding on down the familiar Bristol Road, I lit up at Whitminster and reached the Quarry at 8 o'clock, where I found them just going to bed. Just previous to reaching the Quarry, I became so hungry that I ripped

Photographs taken by Percy Ashworth on two of his expeditions. Place unknown . . .

the top off a brown loaf I had in the haversack and ate it as I came along and it probably tasted better than turtle-soup does to the Lord Mayor. That is where the open-air man gets the pull over the gourmand, at much less expense too. I got to bed about 9 but was so full of events of the previous two days that I did not get to sleep till 1.30. Next morning at 6, however, I was too lively to suit the other occupants of the house, who, at breakfast, requested me not to begin singing so early.

Percy Ashworth.

.....possibly in the Black Mountains (B.J. Ashworth)

The author with his circa 1901, size 3, Dursley Pedersen cycle. (C. Howarth)

Notes on Sources of Information

There is a considerable quantity of retrospective literature on Mikael Pedersen and his cycle, most of it in the form of magazine articles. I confess that much of this I would not have known about without the aid of the circulating 'Pedersen Study Book' of the Southern Veteran-Cycle Club. Some of it is technical in nature and I give references below, and some more general. Though I have not used much, preferring to go where possible to root sources, I acknowledge my indebtedness to the Club and to the contributors for unknowingly suggesting avenues of research.

A great deal of information has come by word of mouth but of written sources the following have been used:—

Major Sources

'*The Dursley Gazette*'

1889	17th August.
1893	21st October; 25th November.
1895	23rd February; 1st June.
1896	21st March; 4th April; 25th April; 21st November; 26th December.
1897	30th January; 27th February; 15th May; 21st August; 28th September.
1898	8th January; 30th April; 21st May; 4th June; 9th July; 20th August; 29th September; 19th November.
1899	25th February; 8th July; 15th July; 12th August; 9th September; 23rd September.
1900	31st March; 30th June; 1st September; 27th October; 24th November; 29th December.
1901	9th February; 25th May; 3rd August; 24th August; 23rd November.
1902	17th May; 19th July; 8th November; 29th November.
1903	10th January; 22nd August; 21st November.
1904	11th June.
1905	18th March; 3rd June; 29th July.

1906	10th March; 28th April; 22nd June; 4th August.
1907	29th June; 6th July; 27th July; 24th August; 30th November; 7th December; 21st December.
1908	8th February; 21st November.
1909	20th February; 27th February; 9th October.
1910	19th November; 3rd December.
1911	23rd September; 25th November.
1912	23rd November.
1913	23rd August; 29th November.
1914	17th January; 12th December.
1915	27th February.
1916	22nd April.

Gloucester Records Office

Documents D 3310. These refer mainly to the period 1902 - 1905 but contain some information about earlier times.

'Implement and Machinery Review'

1890	January page 12580
1893	August page 16909
1902	May page 1430
1907	July page 367
1908	April page 1478; May page 69

'The Motor Cycle'

1913	28th August; 27th November.

Dursley Pedersen Catalogues

Other Sources

'Cycling'   )
C.T.C. 'Gazette'   )   mainly covering the period 1897 - 190(
'The Irish Cyclist')   and 1921 & 1922

Wrights Bristol Directory (Humpage Jacques & Pedersen) 1896 - 1907

Kellys Gloucestershire Directory 1890 - 1920

'The Engineer' 1898 10th June

'Boys Own Paper' 1903 page 651

'Cycling' 1936 12th August (Sidney Swann's Carlisle - London ride)

Technical References

'Cycling' 1938 12th January	'A Bicycle that was Unique' A.C. Davison.
1950 25th May	'The Pedersen Hub' I. Cohen
1956 7th June	'The Stresses of the Dursley Pedersen' I. Cohen.

Index

Italics indicate illustrations